BAWDY VERSE
AND FOLKSONGS

BAWDY VERSE

·AND FOLKSONGS·

written and collected by

ROBERT BURNS

Introduced by

MAGNUS MAGNUSSON

M

MACMILLAN LONDON

This collection first published 1965 by W. H. Allen & Co Ltd
under the title *The Merry Muses of Caledonia.*

This new edition published 1982 by
PAPERMAC
a division of Macmillan Publishers Limited
4 Little Essex Street London WC2R 3LF
and Basingstoke

Associated companies in Auckland, Dallas,
Delhi, Dublin, Hong Kong, Johannesburg,
Lagos, Manzini, Melbourne, Nairobi,
New York, Singapore, Tokyo, Washington
and Zaria

Reprinted 1982

Introduction copyright © Magnus Magnusson 1982

ISBN 0 333 34337 9

Printed in Great Britain by
Redwood Burn Ltd., Trowbridge, Wiltshire and
bound by Pegasus Bookbinding, Melksham, Wiltshire.

NOTE

Punctuation and style in Sections I and VI follow Burns's holograph. Elsewhere, punctuation as a rule follows the text, but where this was very erratic it has sometimes been emended. Inconsistencies in spelling are literal.

CONTENTS

❧❖❧

IV. COLLECTED BY BURNS

INTRODUCTION

❦

BY MAGNUS MAGNUSSON

There was a lad was born in Kyle,
But whatna day o' whatna style
I doubt it's hardly worth the while
    To be sae nice wi' Robin.

Robin was a rovin' boy,
    Rantin' rovin', rantin' rovin';
Robin was a rovin' boy,
    Rantin' rovin' Robin.

Thus Robert Burns—'Robin' to his intimates, 'Rabbie' to posterity—celebrated his birth, "the date of my Bardship's vital existence", in song: 25 January, 1759, in a humble farmer's cottage in the Kyle district of Ayrshire.

It is a boisterous song, one that is lustily rendered at every Burns Night the world over. In it, Burns positively exalts in his reputation as a reveller, a roisterer, a sexual rover. Like so much of Burns' occasional verse it is a neatly-turned conceit. It's hardly worthwhile being precise about the day and circumstances of his birth, he says; what matters is that a godmother (a 'gossip') reads his palm in his cradle and forecasts his future:

This waly boy will be nae coof:
    I think we'll ca' him Robin.

(Translated: This strapping lad will be no dolt, I think we'll call him Robin).

He'll have misfortunes great and small, she says, but always the heart to rise above them all; he'll be a credit to them all, they'll all be proud of him one day:

> He'll hae misfortunes great an' sma',
> But aye a heart aboon them a';
> He'll be a credit till us a',
>   We'll a' be proud of Robin.

More pertinently, she recognises that he is going to be a womaniser: every line of his palm indicates it—so blessings on you, Robin:

> But sure as three times three mak' nine,
> I see by ilka score and line,
> This chap will dearly like our kin',
>   So leeze me on thee, Robin.

The sixth and final stanza of the song used to be omitted by prudish editors as being too specific:

> Guid faith, quo' scho, I doubt you, Sir,
> Ye gar the lasses lie aspar,
> But twenty fauts ye may hae waur,
>   So blessings on thee, Robin!

It was the second line that was too strong for delicate sensibilities: *Ye gar the lasses lie aspar,* "You'll make the girls spread their legs" (though he would have "twenty faults worse than that").

This indecorousness, this down-to-earth robustness of expression, is an integral part of Burns' world-wide appeal. His conspicuous success at making girls "lie aspar" (he fathered at least 14 children, more than half of them illegitimately) is admired and envied, openly or covertly, by most men—and, I suspect, secretly approved by most women. From early puberty he was frankly and outspokenly obsessed with love and sexuality; his very first poem, written at the age of 14, was a love-song to Nellie Kilpatrick, a "bonnie, sweet, sonsie lass" who worked beside him at the harvest, and his very last poem was a love-song to an 18-year-old girl, Jessie Lewars, who helped to nurse him on his death-bed.

But Robert Burns was far more than a mere philanderer; he was far too human, far too ardent and compassionate, to be dismissed as a lewd Lothario. What I find fascinating about Burns as a human being is the intense duality of the man, the contradictions and warring inconsistencies in his character, the dichotomy between the peasant and the poet. It is a duality with which all other human beings can identify. Burns positively exemplified the perpetual human tension between love and lust. All mankind has ever been tormented by this ambiguity; and that is why we can identify so readily with Burns, recognising in him our own failings and our own heady aspirations.

These failings and aspirations were dramatically, indeed spectacularly, juxtaposed during Burns' celebrated "Edinburgh period", when the young country poet went to the Big City to be lionised by the gentry after the publication of the Kilmarnock edition of his early poems.

Picture Robert Burns as he arrives in Edinburgh in November, 1786. He was only 27 years old, and this visit was intended to be a turning-point in his life. He was riding on a borrowed pony. He was wearing a blue coat, a buff waistcoat with broad blue stripes, tight buckskin breeches, and jockey-boots with yellow tops. He wore his hair lank and unpowdered, tied in a short pig-tail. He carried a whip, as if to emphasise his ploughman origins.

What was this farmer's son from Ayrshire doing in Edinburgh, the cultural capital of Scotland? Basically, he was seeking social advancement. He had begun as a local country poet, chronicling the country emotions of "his" people, their loves and hates, their pretensions and realities, their hopes and fears, their work and their play. By now, however, his personal life was in disarray. His father had died, and he was now head of a family struggling to survive in a quagmire of economic difficulties. His love-life was a shambles. He had bedded a local girl, Jean Armour, who bore him twins, then apparently married her secretly, only to have the "marriage" repudiated by the girl's father; he had been publicly humiliated in church for his sins; he was planning to emigrate to Jamaica; he was embroiled with another girl on the rebound, "Highland Mary" Campbell, who seems to have died of fever and/or premature childbirth on her way to meet him at Greenock. Everything was in a total mess. But the spark of survival still glowed fiercely in Burns' heart; he needed money to emigrate, and he had an arrogant belief in his genius as a poet—and so, in April 1786, he persuaded a printer in Kilmarnock to solicit subscriptions for the publication of a volume of *Scotch Poems, by Robert Burns*. "It is the last foolish action that I intend to do", wrote Burns to a friend, "and then turn a wise man as fast as possible." This was the genesis of the Kilmarnock edition of *Poems, Chiefly in the Scottish Dialect*, 240 pages long, containing 34 poems, which was published by the press of John Wilson on July 31, 1786, with a print-run of 612 copies selling at three shillings each.

Its success was immediate and immensely gratifying. It was sold out within a month, both locally and nationally. Burns himself pocketed a modest profit of nearly £20. What mattered much more, however, was that it was well received by the literary critics of Edinburgh. That was enough! Burns abandoned his plans to emigrate (and his grief for "Highland Mary") and set off for Edinburgh in his tight buckskin breeches. His plan was to negotiate a second, much enlarged edition—which was published the following April by William Creech in a print-run of 3,000 copies at five shillings each.

In Edinburgh, Burns enjoyed instant social success. Not long after he arrived, the doyen of Edinburgh *literati*, Henry Mackenzie, author of *The Man of Feeling*, showered praise on him in an article in *The Lounger*:

> Though I am far from meaning to compare our rustic bard to Shakespeare, yet whoever will read his lighter and more humorous poems . . . will perceive with what uncommon penetration and sagacity this Heaven-taught ploughman, from his humble and unlettered station, has looked upon men and manners.

Thus was the myth of Burns as the unlettered, Heaven-taught ploughman poet born. In fact it was totally untrue. Despite his country background, Burns was extremely well educated by the standards of his day. His father had employed a tutor for him, as well as teaching him himself; young Burns had learned French and a little Latin, he had studied both English and Scottish poetry, he read voraciously, he had mastered the gentilities of "Augustan" *belles-lettres* ("posh" writing, we would call it nowadays), and he had a very good, quick mind. Far from being an unlettered peasant, he was by then an extremely well-lettered craftsman.

But Edinburgh wanted him to be a "Heaven-taught ploughman": an interesting social toy to play with, flirt with, patronise, condescend to. Burns was fiercely radical, stridently class-conscious ("The rank is but the guinea's stamp, A man's a man for a' that"), an egalitarian, a reformer, an idealist; but he also had an eye for the main chance, and he knew that Edinburgh could provide him with financial security through official patronage—a sinecure job with the Excise, for instance. So Burns tried to play Edinburgh at its own game: if Edinburgh wanted a Heaven-taught ploughman, a Heaven-taught ploughman it would get.

This was the public role that Robert Burns deliberately assumed for the drawing-rooms of Edinburgh. He emphasised it shamelessly in his Dedication for the Edinburgh edition of his poems in April, 1787:

> The Poetic Genius of my Country found me as the prophetic bard Elijah did Elisha—at the *plough*, and threw her inspiring mantle over me. She bade me sing the loves, the joys, the rural scenes and rural pleasures of my native Soil, in my native tongue: I tuned my wild, artless notes, as she inspired.

Burns undoubtedly enjoyed all the lionising, although he resented the condescension. The *literati* earnestly advised him to write more in English, less in Scots, and Burns duly obliged with appalling stilted poems like *Address to Edinburgh*, which begins "Edina! Scotia's darling seat, All hail thy palaces and tow'rs . . ." and was solemnly added to the 1787 edition. They were less enthusiastic about the rumbustious dialect humour of his *Address to a Haggis:*

> Fair fa' your honest, sonsie face,
> Great chieftain o' the puddin-race!
> Aboon them a' ye tak your place,
>   Painch, tripe or thairm:
> Weel are ye wordy o' a grace
>   As lang's my arm.

The ladies of Edinburgh were entranced by the smouldering passion they knew was lurking within him, the roughness beneath the polite exterior. One gossip wrote to a friend: "The town is at present agog with the ploughman poet, who receives adulation with native dignity, and is the very figure of his profession—strong and coarse—but has a most enthusiastic heart of LOVE.''

It was all a front. Burns at that time was lodging in what was little better than a brothel in Baxter's Close in the Lawnmarket for 18 pence a week. While he was dancing attendance on rich and beautiful women like the giddy Duchess of Gordon, and Lord Monboddo's daughter Elizabeth Burnet, his alter ago, the other Burns, the real Burns, was enjoying an Edinburgh servant girl, May Cameron, who bore him an illegitimate child.

On his second visit to Edinburgh, the following winter, after a leisurely tour of the Highlands and the Borders to collect songs, the pattern was repeated. He threw himself into an extraordinarily ardent affair, much of it by correspondence, with a well-born and voluptuous Edinburgh grass-widow called Nancy M'Lehose, whose ne'er-do-well husband had deserted her. They called one another by the pastoral names of ''Clarinda'' and ''Sylvander''—masks of Arcadian innocence; Sir Walter Scott, who as a boy met Burns briefly in an Edinburgh salon, later said of their letters that they were ''the most extraordinary mixture of sense and nonsense, and of love human and divine, that was ever exposed to the eye of the world.''

Nancy did her best to conduct the affair at arm's length; but behind the mask of genteel sensibility and purity of thought, Burns' physical desire for her was becoming more and more urgent. She was playing with fire, and she knew it, as one of her verses to him reveals:

> Talk not of Love, it gives me pain,
>   For Love has been my foe;
> He bound me with an iron chain,
>   And plunged me deep in woe . . .
>
> Your Friendship much can make me blest,
>   O, why that bliss destroy!
> Why urge the odious, one request
>   You know I must deny!

At the same time as Burns was pouring out his protestations of love to Nancy, he himself was busy bedding yet another Edinburgh servant-girl, Jenny Clow, who also bore him an illegitimate child; and back in Ayrshire his "secret" wife, Jean Armour, was pregnant once again, the result of a clandestine meeting that summer. Soon even Burns found his Jekyll-and-Hyde Edinburgh existence insupportable, and in February, 1788, he left the city for Ayrshire after a final flurry of letters and meetings with Nancy. She seems to have escaped with her virtue and reputation more or less intact; yet it had clearly been a bruising experience for them both. Three years later she was to be rewarded with a memorable love-song:

> Ae fond kiss, and then we sever!
> Ae farewell, and then forever!
> Deep in heart-wrung tears I'll pledge thee,
> Warring sighs and groans I'll wage thee . . .

> Had we never lov'd sae kindly,
> Had we never lov'd sae blindly,
> Never met—or never parted—
> We had ne'er been broken-hearted.

There is another footnote to the Clarinda affair which luridly highlights the astonishing duality of Burns' personality. As soon as he returned to Ayrshire he went to see Jean Armour, who was by then eight months pregnant; thereafter he wrote two letters which are so indecently contradictory as to be shocking. To Nancy M'Lehose, the Sylvander in Burns wrote:

Now for a little news that will please you. I, this morning as I came home, called for a certain woman. I am disgusted with her; I cannot endure her! I, while my heart smote me for the profanity, tried to compare her with my Clarinda: 'twas setting the expiring glimmer of a farthing taper beside the cloudless glory of meridian sun. Here was tasteless insipidity, vulgarity of soul, and mercenary fawning; there polished good sense, heaven-born genius, and the most generous, the most delicate, the most tender Passion. I have done with her, and she with me!

But to one of his Edinburgh drinking companions, the other Burns wrote of the meeting in a very different vein—earthy, vulgar, sexually boastful:

Jean I found banished like a martyr—forlorn, destitute and friendless; all for the good old cause: I have reconciled her to her fate: I have reconciled her to her mother: I have taken her a room: I have taken her to my arms: I have given her a mahogany bed: I have given her a guinea; and I have f - - - d her till she rejoiced with joy unspeakable and full of glory. But—as I always am on every occasion—-I have been prudent and cautious to an astounding degree; I swore her, privately and solemnly, never to attempt any claim on me as a husband, even though anybody should persuade her she had such a claim, which she has not, neither during my life or after my death. She did all this like a good girl, and I took the opportunity of some dry horselitter, and gave her such a thundering scalade that electrified the very marrow of her bones.

Not surprisingly, Jean Armour gave birth prematurely after all these excitements—a second set of twins, who both died within a few weeks. But despite the protestations in both his earlier letters, Burns *did* in fact marry Jean Armour only a few days later. She was to bear him nine children in all (the last on the day of his funeral in 1796), only three of whom survived him.

Nothing can exemplify more starkly the crude duality of the Burns *persona* than the Edinburgh period of his life and all its ramifications. But before we judge him too harshly, let us remember how we ourselves would shudder if all of our own private thoughts and actions were ever to be examined with the appalling clarity that Burns has had to endure posthumously. What terrible imperfections would not be revealed? What large and little shames? What disgraceful gulfs between public attitudes and private actions, between romantic ideals and mundane deeds, between aspirations and achievements? Poor Burns has suffered from the fact that we know such a great deal about him. In the days before the telephone (and the birth pill), he committed himself to life, to experience, to passion, with uncompromising immediacy and ardour. Every thought that ever passed through his head, it seems, was chronicled and recorded. How many of us could stand up to that kind of scrutiny?

And because we are all human ourselves, we can expiate our own feelings of guilt through Burns, consoling ourselves with the awareness of his other, compensatory qualities. We can admire the sheer ardour with which the man lived, for ardour is not a very common quality nowadays. Nor is compassion. Nor is romantic idealism. Nor is the gift of simple lyricism. To all these facets of life he brought a tremendous vitality, as generous and energetic as that great narrative poem (which he composed in a single day) *Tam o' Shanter*, with its galloping, rollicking pace and rhythm, or as gleeful and full-blooded as his splendid verse Satires on human frailties and hypocrisies like *Holy Willie's Prayer* and *The Holy Fair*.

For these and other towering masterpieces of his genius for the raw stuff of humanity we forgive him all. He was, in his way, the original Angry Young Man; but his was the anger of compassion, not the bitter, inward-looking anger of self-pity, never cheap or sneering. He championed a more liberal and tolerant outlook on life—for others as well as for himself—tilting strenuously against the strict Calvinist preachings of 18th century Presbyterians with their belief in original sin and predestined retribution.

It comes across with appealing impact in many of his simpler poems ("naive" is the fashionable word for them). In *To a Mouse*, for instance, he identifies movingly with a little creature of the fields whose laboriously-constructed nest he has unwittingly shattered with his plough, and finds in that tiny episode a parable for all mankind:

> But Mousie, thou art no thy lane,   [alone]
> In proving foresight may be vain:
> The best-laid schemes o' mice an' men
> Gang aft agley,
> An' lea'e us nought but grief an' pain,
> For promis'd joy!

That one superb line—*The best-laid schemes of mice and men gang aft agley*—is perhaps the best-known in the Burns corpus; it's little wonder that John Steinbeck plundered it for his magnificent novel, *Of Mice and Men*. Burns had a rare facility for making the commonplace memorable, and the platitude profound. He also had a certain fondness for sentimental moralizing and democratic cant (Hugh MacDairmid once said of him that he "wrote mush for the masses much of the time"); but that is what has made him, *par excellence*, the poet of humanity, the poet of mankind. That is what helps to explain the remarkable phenomenon of the world-wide Burns Cult. It is not so much his philosophy as our own capacity for self-deception that we celebrate at Burns Nights: humanity caught in the act.

One aspect of this "caught-in-the-act" humanity is celebrated in the verses in this volume. This collection of indecorous verse is one of the spin-offs of his Edinburgh period. It is an anthology of bawdy songs and poems that would nowadays be justified as "Rugby Songs", although they are considerably less smutty and crude than that.

While Burns was in Edinburgh he was made a member of a convivial drinking-club known as "The Crochallan Fencibles", which met regularly in a tavern in Anchor Close run by Daniel Douglas, a celebrated inn-keeper of his day. It was a fairly "up-market" sort of club, socially, and since the tavern was close to Parliament House in Edinburgh, the legal fraternity was prominent in its membership. The name of the club is supposed to have been derived from two elements: the Gaelic song *Crodh Chailean* ("Colin's Cattle"), which the inn-keeper was fond of singing, and the current practice of forming volunteer militia corps, or "fencibles", at the time of the American War of Independence. The club met regularly and frequently for evenings of hard drinking and cheerful company; Robert Burns, with his wit and his gaiety and what he himself called his "violent propensity to bawdy", quickly became a leading spirit.

For his like-minded companions in "The Crochallan Fencibles" Burns provided a steady supply of bawdy ballads and indecent songs which he had been collecting and composing for years. Scholars have argued mightily about the provenance of these poems, which were published from private manuscripts in a pirate edition in 1800 as *The Merry Muses of Caledonia;* but it is generally agreed that he was the author of at least half of them and the editor/collector of nearly all the rest.

They are in no way pornographic, these songs and poems. They are not "dirty" or prurient-minded. They are frank, vigorous, indiscreet, witty and clever. Above all they are a joyous celebration of sex in all its splendour and absurdity. Like so much of Burns' work, they combine social comment with devastating satire on sexual hypocrisy.

They are to be read for fun, for enjoyment, for laughs, as they were undoubtedly received by "The Crochallan Fencibles".

They are memorials to a robust tradition of vernacular folk-song which has always flourished in Scotland.

I welcome this volume. It is only in recent years that the original 1800 edition (of which only one precious copy has survived, in private ownership) has been rescued by scholarship, meticulously edited, and re-issued. Once they were hardly thought fit to print—Burns himself never intended them to be published; apologists for Burns, over-zealous to protect his reputation, either bowdlerised them, suppressed them, or denied his authorship of them.

We live in a less constrained society now, one in which the value of bawdry as a social and sexual safety-valve is recognised. Risqué jokes are now acceptable in polite, mixed company as long as they are clever rather than blue. But whatever the literary or poetic merit of these bawdy ballads of Burns, they are indispensable to a proper understanding of the poet and his many-sided personality. Lord Byron summed it up perfectly in a comment in his Journal, after reading some of them in Burns' then unpublished letters:

> What an antithetical mind!—tenderness, roughness—delicacy, coarseness—sentiment, sensuality—soaring and grovelling, dirt and deity—all mixed up in that one compound of inspired clay!

GLOSSARY

A', *all*
Abee, *me be*
Aboon, *above*
Ae, *one*
Aff, *off*
Aften, *often*
Again, *against*
Aiblens, *perhaps*
Aik, *an oak*
Ain, *own*
Airt, *direction; to direct*
Aith, *an oath*
Aits, *oats*
Alane, *alone*
An, *if*
Ance, *once*
Ane, *one*
An's, *and is; and his*
Arle, *pledge*
Arselins, *backwards*
As due as, *whenever*
Atweesh, *between*
Awa, *away*
Awe, *to owe*
Awee, *a little time*
Ayont, *beyond*

Bad, *bid*
Bade, *endured; desired; persuaded*
Bairn'd, *got with child*
Baith, *both*
Bann'd, *cursed*
Bane, *bone*
Bang, *a stroke*
Bauld, *bold*
Bawsent, *white-streaked on face*
Be, *by*
Bear, *barley*
Bed-stock, *bedside; wooden bar at front of box bed*
Befa', *befall*
Behint, *behind*
Belang, *belong to*

Beld, *bald*
Belyve, *by and by*
Ben, *inside; the inner room*
Bends, *bounds*
Bent, *coarse grass near sea*
Be't, *be it*
Bicker, *beaker; move quickly*
Bide, *to stand, to endure*
Bien (of a person), *well-to-do; (of a place), comfortable*
Bigget, biggit, *built*
Birkie, *fellow*
Birss, *hair; bristle*
Blatter, *attack*
Blaw, *to blow; to brag*
Bleerie, *bleary-eyed; small beer*
Blin', *blind*
Blooster, *bluster*
Blyth, *happily*
Bock, *to spew; to vomit*
Boddle, *one-sixth of a penny*
Boost, *must needs*
Bort, *bored*
Bousing, *drinking*
Bowe, *bowl*
Brae, *slope of a hill*
Braid, *cloth*
Brak, *did break*
Braulies, *splendidly*
Braw, *fine; handsome*
Brawly's, *finely as*
Broads, *shutters*
Brose, *porridge*
Browst, *a brewing*
Brunt, *burnt*
Brust, *burst*
Buckl'd, *curled*
Busk, *bush; dress*
Buskit, *dressed; decked*
But(t), *without; wanting; only; outer room*
Buttock-hire, *penance*
Byke, *hive*

Byre-en', *cowshed end*

Ca', *to drive; call; summon*
Ca' throu', *to push forward*
Cadger, *a carrier*
Caller, *fresh*
Cam, *came*
Cameronian, *Presbyterian sect*
Canie, *careful*
Canty, *cheerful*
Carl, *a man*
Carlin, *an old woman*
Cauld, *cold*
Chap, *to knock*
Chaup, *a blow*
Chiel, *young fellow*
Chitterling, *shirt frill*
Chuckies, *chickens*
Claes, *clothes; covers*
Clag, *burden*
Claise, *clothes*
Claith, *cloth*
Clamb, *climbed*
Clappin', *fondling*
Clash, *gossip; to talk*
Clatter, *to talk idly; gossip*
Claught, *clutched*
Claut, *rake*
Claw, *to scratch; to fondle*
Cleek, *hook*
Clegs, *spurs*
Clew, *scratched; fondled*
Clishmaclavers, *idle talk*
Clocken-hen, *broody hen*
Cloot, *hoof*
Clout, *mend; patch*
Clouts, *clothes*
Clue, *cleuch, narrow glen*
Coal-riddle, *sieve*
Coft, *bought*
Coggin', *wedging*
Cogie, *a small wooden pail*
Coof, *a fool*
Coost, *did cast off*
Coost out, *quarrelled*
Coup, *to overturn; a fall*
Courtha', *court hall*
Cow, *coward*
Cowe, *to crop; to subdue; horror*
Cow'd, *cropped*
Crack, *gossip*
Crap, *crept; a crop*

Craw, *to crow*
Creel, *a basket*
Crowdie, *curds; cheese*
Cuttie, *little*
Cuttie-gun, *short tobacco pipe*
Cuttie-mun, *old song*
Cuttie stoup, *short drinks*

Dae, *do*
Daffin, *sporting*
Dang, *pushed; knocked*
Darge, *day's work*
Daud, *a lump; a large piece*
Daunton, *awe*
Daur, *dare*
Dawtin', *petting*
Deevil's dizzen, *13 inches*
Deil, *the devil*
Dibble, *tool*
Ding, *to shove; to hit*
Dinna, *do not*
Ditty, *indictment*
Dizzen, *dozen*
Docht, *could*
Dock, *tail*
Dockins, *dock leaves*
Dod, *jog*
Doit, *mite*
Dool, *a blow; sorrowful*
Doudled, *dandled*
Dought na, *dared not*
Dow, *do; can*
Dow, *a pigeon*
Downa-do, *old age*
Down-cod, *feather pillow*
Draik, *to soak*
Dree, *to bear; to endure*
Dreep, *to drip*
Druken, *drunken*
Dud, Duddie, *ragged*
Duntie, *thump*
Dunts, *strokes; blows; knocks*
Durk, *a dagger*
Dyke-back, *back of the wall*

Eastlin, *eastern*
Ee, *eye; to watch*
Een or **ein**, *eyes*
Eith, *easy*
Elekit, *of the Elect*
En', *end*

Fa', *enjoy; fall*
Fae, *foe*
Fa'en, *fallen*
Fairin', *food*
Fand, *found*
Fash, *heed*
Fash'd, *vexed*
Fauld, *folded; a fold*
Fauteors a', *offenders all*
Fau't, *fault*
Fau'tor, *offender*
Fauts, *faults*
Fee, *wage; to hire*
Feetie, *feet*
Fidge, *to exert*
Fient a, *devil a*
Fin', *find*
Fistles, *fizzes; fidgets*
Fit, *foot*
Fit-man, *footman*
Fitstead, *footstep*
Flaes, *fleas; flies*
Flang, *struggled; heaved; flung*
Flate, *protested*
Fley'd, *afraid*
Flowe, *morass*
Fly'd, *frightened*
Flytin, *scolding*
Fodgel'd, *heaved; shook*
Foggie, *mossy*
Foot, *speed*
Forbye, *besides*
Forgat, *forgot*
Fou, *full; drunk*
Frae, *from*
Fu', *full; drunk*
Fun', *found*
Fur *or* furr, *furrow*
Fyke, *fidget; bustle*

Gae, *go; gave*
Gaed *or* gade, *went*
Gager, gauger, *exciseman*
Gain', *against*
Gair, *gusset*
Gamon, *petticoat; legs*
Gang, *to go*
Gar, *to make; to compel; to cause to*
Gard, *past tense of* Gar
Garse, *grass*
Gart it clink, *made it chime*
Gart me, *got me to*

Gat, *got*
Gate, *road*
Gaud, *goad*
Gaun, *going*
Gavel, *gable*
Gear, *wealth, goods; harness*
Gerse, *grass*
Gets, *children; brats*
Gie, *give*
Gied me the glaiks, *jilted me*
Gif, *if*
Gin, *if*
Girdin', *driving; exercise*
Girt, *girded; girth; large*
Gizzen, *dry up*
Glaur, *muck, mud*
Gled, *buzzard; kite*
Glowran, *gazing*
Goosset, *gusset*
Goud *or* gowd, *gold*
Gowan, *daisies*
Graipit, *groped; examined; searched*
Graith, *equipment; gear*
Grane, *groan*
Grat, *wept*
Gravat, *muffler*
Greetie, *crying*
Gripet, *grasped*
Groazle, *grunt*
Gully, *cut; stab; poke*
Gyvel *or* gyvle, *hind parts; gable*

Ha', *hall*
Had, *hold*
Hae, *have*
Hadin', *leading*
Haen, *had*
Hafflins, *partially; halfway*
Hair, *corn*
Haith, *faith!*
Haly, *holy*
Haly band, *kirk session*
Hame, *home*
Han', *hand*
Hanger, *dagger*
Hard, *heard*
Haud, *hold*
Hawkie, *white faced cow*
Heigh, *high*
Her lane, *alone; by herself*
Herryin', *robbing*
Hie, *high*

Hing, *hang*
Hinnie, *honey*
Hissie *or* hizzie, *girl ;* hussie
Holland-sark, *linen shift*
Hotch, *shove ; jerk*
Hough, *thigh*
Houghmagandie, *fornication*
Hoven, *swollen*
Howe, *hollow*
Howk, *dig*
Hoy'd, *hailed*
Hurchin, *hedgehog*
Hurdies, *buttocks*
Hurdies fyke, *buttocks in action*
Hurly, *storm*

Ilk, ilka, *each, every*
Ither, *each one ; other*
Ither, *adder*
Its lane, *by itself*
I's no, *I'll not*
Itsel, *itself*

Jad, *a jade*
Jander, *to chatter*
Jimp, *slender, neat*
Jink, *to dodge*
Jirts, *jerks*
Jo, *sweetheart ; joy*

Kail, *soup ; broth*
Kecklin, *cackling*
Keep out, *watch out*
Ken, *know*
Kend, *knew ; known*
Kill, *kiln*
Kimmer, *woman, girl, wench*
Kimmerland, *womankind*
Kintra, *country*
Kipples, *coupling*
Kirst'nin', *christening*
Kittle, *ticklish, difficult ; danger-
 ous ; tricky*
Knocking-stone, *stone mortar for
 hulling barley*
Knowe, *knoll ; hillock*
Koontrie, *country*
Kye, *cattle*
Kytch, *toss*
Kyvle, *tumble*

Labour lee, *plough grassland*

Labster, *lobster*
Laft, *loft*
Laigh, *low*
Laik, *lack*
Lair, *bog*
Laithron doup, *lazy rump*
Lane, *alone (see* Her 1., Its 1.*)*
Lang's, *long as*
Langsyne saunts, *saints of long ago*
Lap, *leapt*
Lat, *let*
Lave, *the rest*
Laverock, *the lark*
Lea's, *leaves*
Lee-rig, *untilled field*
Leuch *or* leugh, *laughed*
Licket, *have licked*
Lien, *lain*
Liltit, *pulled*
Linkin', *sprightly*
Links, *locks*
Loan, *lane*
Lo'e, loo, *love*
Loon, loun, *fellow ; lad*
Loot, *let (past)*
Loups, *leaps*
Lous'd, *loosened*
Louse, *to loosen*
Lowe, *blaze*
Lown, *lad*
Lowse, *to loosen, let loose*
Lucky, *goodwife ; alewife*
Lug, *to pull*
Lugs, *ears*

Mae, *more*
Mail, *meal ; male*
Mair, *more*
Maist, *almost ; most*
Mak, *make*
Make, *like, equal, peer*
Mallison, *curse*
Mane, *moan*
Mantie, *cloth*
Margh, *marrow*
Ma't, *malt*
Maukin, *a hare*
Maun, *must*
Maunna, *must not*
Meal-pocks, *meal bags*
Meikle, *much*
Mess, *minister*

Midden wa', *dunghill wall*
Mim-mou'd, *mealymouthed*
Minnie, *mother*
Misca'd, *abused*
Modeworck *or* modiewark, *mole*
Mou', *mouth*
Moulie, *soft; earthy*
Mowe, *copulate*
Muckle, *big; much*
Muir, *moor*

Naething, *nothing*
Naigs, *nags*
Na mony, *few*
Nane, *none*
Neebor, *neighbour*
Neep, *turnip*
Neist *or* niest, *next*
Neive *or* nieve, *fist*
Nerse, *tail*
Nicher, *whinny; snigger*
Nidge't, *squeezed*
Nine, *nine inches long*
Nits, *nuts*
Nocht, *nothing*
Nyvel, *navel*

Onie *or* ony, *any*
Or, *before*
O't, *of it*
Ousen, *oxen*
Owsen-staw, *ox stall*

Pat, *put*
Pat it in my will, *gave me my way*
Pegh, *puff*
Pickle, *little; grain of corn*
Pickle hair, *last corn cut*
Pillie, *male organ*
Pintle, *pipe; male organ*
Pit, *put*
Pith, *strength*
Plack, *a third of a penny*
Playing bye, *being false to*
Pock, *bag*
Pockie, *small sac*
Poosion, *poison*
Pounie, pownie, *pony*
Pow, *the head; to pull*
Prie, *to accept; to taste*
Pry, *to try; to taste*
Pu'd, *pulled*

Quarter, *one-quarter yard; 9 inches*
Quech, *two-eared cup*
Quine, *lass; wench*
Quo', *quoth*

Raep, *rope*
Rair, *roar*
Rase, *rose*
Rash, *a rush*
Raxin, *reaching*
Ream, *foam*
Rede, *advise*
Reek, *smoke*
Rig, *field, ridge, furrow*
Ring, *reign*
Ripples, *backache*
Rive, *tear*
Roaring-pin, *rolling pin*
Rock, *a distaff*
Rough, *plentiful*
Roughness, *brushwood*
Row, *roll up; wrap*
Rowted, *bellowed*
Rowth, *plenty*
Rug, *tug*
Runt, *cabbage stalk*

Sae, *so*
Saft, *soft*
Sair, *to serve; sore; sorely; severe;*
   very much
Saird, *served*
Sairest, *hardest*
Sangs, *songs*
Sark, *shift; shirt; chemise*
Sa'tty, *salty*
Saunt, *saint*
Scauld, *scold*
Scauls, *scolds*
Sclates, *slates*
Sel, *self*
Sell'd, *sold*
Shaw, *show*
Sheds, *divides, parts, separates*
Sherra, *sheriff*
Shillin hill, *winnowing hill*
Shoen, shoon, *shoes*
Sic, *such*
Siccan a, *such a*
Sicker, *sure*
Side and wide, *large and low-hung*

Siller, *money ; silver*
Sin, *since*
Sinnens, *sinews*
Sinsyne, *since then*
Skelpit doup, *slapped rump*
Sma', *small ; thin*
Sock, *ploughshare*
Sodger, soger *or* sojer, *soldier*
Sonsy, *lively, blooming, hale*
Soud, *should*
Souple, *yielding ; to make supple ; to soak*
Sowen-pat, *gruel pot*
Spak, *spoke*
Speel, *climb*
Spier, *ask*
Spretty bush, *clump of rushes*
Stane, *stone*
Stane o' stanin' graith, *set of good equipment*
Stang, *sting*
Stanin', *standing ; hesitantly*
Stan't themlane, *stood by themselves*
Stark, *strong*
Starns, *stars*
Staund, *set*
Staunin', *standing ; erect*
Steer, *stir ; arouse*
Stell'd, *braced*
Sten, *leap*
Stented graith, *harnessed the plough*
Steward, *housekeeper*
Stibble, *stubble*
Stilts, *shafts*
Stown't, *stolen it*
Strack, *struck*
Straik, *stroke*
Straik o't, *shot at it*
Strang, *strong*
Strunt, *spirits*
Succar, succour, *sugar ; sugary*
Swats, *small beer*
Sykie risk, *watery marsh*
Syne, *then ; since*

Tae, *too ; to ; toe*
Taen, *taken*
Tald, *told*
Taper, *shapely*
Tappit hen, *jug containing a Scots quart* (=3 *English quarts*)

Tell'd, *told*
Tent, *attend*
Term-day, *Whitsunday ; Martinmas*
Tham, *them*
Theekit, *thatched*
Thegither, *together*
Thie, *thigh*
Thirl, *thrill*
Thole, *endure*
Thrang, *full ; thronged*
Thrave, 24 *sheaves of grain*
Thretty, *thirty*
Thumpin, *buxom*
Tight, *shapely, trim, sound*
Tither, *t'other*
Till, *to*
Till't, *tilled ; "went to it"*
Tinkler, *tinker*
Tine, tint, *lose, lost*
Tirliewirlies, *ornaments*
Tittling, *sparrow*
Titty, *sister*
Tocher, *dowry*
Todlen, *toddling*
Toop-horn, *ram's horn*
Touzle, *dishevel*
Trams, *shafts*
Trogger, *a pedlar*
Trow, *to swear ; believe*
Trow'd, *rolled over*
True, *to believe, to trust*
Twa, *two*
Twalt, *twelfth*
Tway thumb-bread, *two thumbs' breadth*
Twynin', *weaving ; parting*

Unco, *uncommon ; great ; strange*
Unkenned, *unknown*

Vera, *very*
Verra crack, *instant*

Wa', *a wall*
Wad, *would ; would have ; wed*
Wae gae by, *woe to*
Waes me, *alas, woe is me*
Waft, *to weave ; weft or woof*
Waigles, *waggles*
Wakin', *walking*
Waled, *picked*

Waly, *well*
Wame, *belly*
Wan, *won*
Want, *lack; lose*
Wants the, *has no*
Wap, *wrap*
Wark, *work*
Warld, *world*
Warst, *worst*
Wast, *west*
Wat, *to know; wet*
Wauken'd, *wakened*
Waukin, *awake*
Waulies, *the buttocks*
Waur, *worse*
Waur't, *worried*
Waxen wan, *grown feeble*
Wean, *child*
Wearin', *using*
Weary fa', *curses on*
Webster, *weaver*
Wee, *little; a bit; a short period of time*
Wee coat, *petticoat*
Weel, *well*
Weel-knoozed, *well-kneaded*
Weet, *splash-board; wet*

Weetin', *wetting*
Weir, *war; might*
Whang, *tape; lace; a large slice*
Whatreck, *weasel*
What she could bicker, *as fast as she could*
Whiltie-whaltie, *in a state of palpitation*
Whittle, *knife*
Whyles, *sometimes*
Wight, *brisk*
Wi little wark, *easily*
Wimble bores, *small holes*
Win', *wind*
Windy-wa's, *windy walls; a boaster*
Winna, *will not*
Wordy, *worthy*
Wyte, *blame*

Yeard, *yard*
Yerk, *to drive; to jerk*
Ye'se, *you shall; you will*
Yill, *ale*
Yin, *one*
Yokin', *a stint; a bout*
Yorlin, *a finch; yellow hammer*

I

❧

FROM BURNS'
MANUSCRIPTS

[The verses in this section are taken
from the authentic Burns'
manuscripts; the bulk of the rest of
the book is taken from the collection
originally published as *The Merry
Muses of Caledonia* in 1880.]

A. *By Burns*

I'LL TELL YOU A TALE OF A WIFE

TUNE: *Auld Sir Symon*

❀❖❀

I'll tell you a tale of a Wife,
   And she was a Whig and a Saunt;
She liv'd a most sanctify'd life,
   But whyles she was fash'd wi' her ——.——
     Fal lal &c.

2

Poor woman! she gaed to the Priest,
   And till him she made her complaint;
"There's naething that troubles my breast
   "Sae sair as the sins o' my ——.——

3

"Sin that I was herdin at hame,
   "Till now I'm three score & ayont,
"I own it wi' sin & wi' shame
   "I've led a sad life wi' my ——.——

4

He bade her to clear up her brow,
   And no be discourag'd upon 't;
For holy gude women enow
   Were mony times waur't wi' their ——.——

5

It's naught but Beelzebub's art,
   But that's the mair sign of a saunt,
He kens that ye're pure at the heart,
   Sae levels his darts at your ——.——

6

What signifies Morals & Works,
    Our works are no wordy a runt!
It's Faith that is sound, orthodox
    That covers the fauts o' your ——.—

7

Were ye o' the Reprobate race
    Created to sin & be brunt,
O then it would alter the case
    If ye should gae wrang wi' your ——.—

8

But you that is Called & Free
    Elekit & chosen a saunt,
Will't break the Eternal Decree
    Whatever ye do wi' your ——?—

9

And now with a sanctify'd kiss
    Let's kneel & renew covenant:
It's this—and it's this—and it's this—
    That settles the pride o' your ——.—

10

Devotion blew up to a flame;
    No words can do justice upon't;
The honest auld woman gaed hame
    Rejoicing and clawin her ——.—

Then high to her memory charge;
   And may he who takes it affront,
Still ride in Love's channel at large,
   And never make port in a ——!!!

BONIE MARY

TUNE: *Minnie's ay glowering o'er me—*

❧❖❧

Chorus—

Come cowe me, minnie, come cowe me;
Come cowe me, minnie, come cowe me;
The hair o' my a— is grown into my c—t,
And they canna win too [*sic*], to m—we me.

1

When Mary cam over the Border,
When Mary cam over the Border;
As eith 'twas approachin the C—t of a hurchin,
Her a— was in sic a disorder.—

2

But wanton Wattie cam west on't,
But wanton Wattie cam west on't,
He did it sae tickle, he left nae as meikle
'S a spider wad bigget a nest on't.—

3

And was nae Wattie a Clinker,
He m—w'd frae the Queen to the tinkler
Then sat down, in grief, like the Macedon chief
For want o' mae warlds to conquer.—

4

And O, what a jewel was Mary!
And O, what a jewel was Mary!
Her face it was fine, & her bosom divine,
And her c—nt it was theekit wi' glory.—

Come cowe &c.

ACT SEDERUNT OF THE SESSION

TUNE: *O'er the muir among the heather*

⌒◈⌒

A Scots Ballad—

In Edinburgh town they've made a law,
   In Edinburgh at the Court o' Session
That standing pr—cks are fauteors a',
   And guilty of a high transgression.—

   Chorus

Act Sederunt o' the Session,
Decreet o' the Court o' Session,
That standing pr—cks are fauteors a',
And guilty of a high transgression.

2

And they've provided dungeons deep.
   Ilk lass has ane in her possession;
Untill the wretches wail and weep,
   They there shall lie for their transgression.—

   Chorus

Act Sederunt o' the Session,
Decreet o' the Court o' Session,
The rogues in pouring tears shall weep,
By act Sederunt o' the Session.—

WHEN PRINCES AND PRELATES

TUNE: *The Campbells are Coming*

⌒◈⌒

When princes & prelates & het-headed zealots
    All Europe hae set in a lowe,
The poor man lies down, nor envies a crown,
    And comforts himself with a mowe.—

        Chorus—

    And why shouldna poor folk mowe, mowe, mowe,
        And why shouldna poor folk mowe:
    The great folk hae siller, & houses & lands,
        Poor bodies hae naething but mowe.—

2

When Br—nsw—ck's great Prince cam a cruising to
    Fr—nce,
    Republican billies to cowe,
Bauld Br—nsw—ck's great Prince wad hae shawn
    better sense,
    At hame with his Princess to mowe.—
And why should na &c.

3

Out over the Rhine proud Pr—ss—a wad shine,
    To *spend* his best blood he did vow;
But Frederic had better ne'er forded the water,
    But spent as he docht in a mowe.—
And why &c.

4

By sea & by shore! the Emp—r—r swore,
    In Paris he'd kick up a row;

But Paris sae ready just leugh at the laddie
   And bade him gae tak him a mowe.—
And why &c.

5

Auld Kate laid her claws on poor Stanislaus,
   And Poland has bent like a bow:
May the deil in her a— ram a huge pr—ck o' brass!
   And damn her in h—ll with a mowe!

6

But truce with commotions & new-fangled notions,
   A bumper I trust you'll allow:
Here's George our gude king & Charlotte his queen
   And lang may they tak a gude mowe!

WHILE PROSE-WORK AND RHYMES

TUNE: *The Campbells Are Coming*

❖

A Ballad

While Prose-work & rhymes
   Are hunted for crimes,
And things are—the devil knows how;
   Aware o' my rhymes,
   In these kittle times,
The subject I chuse is a ——.

Some cry, Constitution!
   Some cry, Revolution!
And Politics kick up a rowe;
   But Prince & Republic,
   Agree on the Subject,
No treason is in a good ——.

Th' Episcopal lawn,
   And Presbyter band,
Hae lang been to ither a cowe;
   But still the proud Prelate,
   And Presbyter zealot
Agree in an orthodox ——.

Poor Justice, 'tis hinted—
   Ill natur'dly squinted,
The Process—but mum—we'll allow—
   Poor Justice has ever
   For C—t had a favor,
While Justice could tak a gude ——.

Now fill to the brim—
    To her, & to him,
Wha willingly do what they dow;
    And ne'er a poor wench
    Want a friend at a pinch,
Whase failing is only a ——.

NINE INCH WILL PLEASE A LADY

To its ain tune—

◦◈◦

1

"Come rede me, dame, come tell me, dame,
   "My dame come tell me truly,
"What length o' graith, when weel ca'd hame,
   "Will sair a woman duly?"
The carlin clew her wanton tail,
   Her wanton tail sae ready—
I learn'd a sang in Annandale,
   Nine inch will please a lady.—

2

But for a koontrie c—nt like mine,
   In sooth, we're nae sae gentle;
We'll tak tway thumb-bread to the nine,
   And that's a sonsy p—ntle:
O Leeze me on * my Charlie lad,
   I'll ne'er forget my Charlie!
Tway roarin handfu's and a daud,
   He nidge't it in fu' rarely.—

3

But weary fa' the laithron doup,
   And may it ne'er be thrivin!
It's no the length that maks me loup,
   But it's the double drivin.—
Come nidge me, Tam, come nudge me, Tam,
   Come nidge me o'er the nyvel!
Come lowse & lug your battering ram,
   And thrash him at my gyvel!

* *Leeze me on;* untranslatable expression denoting great pleasure in or affection for a person or thing.

ODE TO SPRING

TUNE: *The tither morn*

⭗◈⭗

When maukin bucks, at early f——s,
   In dewy grass are seen, Sir;
And birds, on boughs, take off their m——s,
   Amang the leaves sae green, Sir;
Latona's son looks liquorish on
   Dame Nature's grand impètus,
Till his p—go rise, then westward flies
   To r—ger Madame Thetis.

Yon wandering rill that marks the hill,
   And glances o'er the brae, Sir,
Glides by a bower where many a flower
   Sheds fragrance on the day, Sir;
There Damon lay, with Sylvia gay,
   To love they thought no crime, Sir;
The wild-birds sang, the echoes rang,
   While Damon's a—se beat time, Sir.——

First, wi' the thrush, his thrust & push
   Had compass large & long, Sir;
The blackbird next, his tuneful text,
   Was bolder, clear & strong, Sir;
The linnet's lay came then in play,
   And the lark that soar'd aboon, Sir;
Till Damon, fierce, mistim'd his a——,
   And f——'d quite out of tune, Sir.——

O SAW YE MY MAGGIE?

TUNE: *O Saw ye na my Peggy?*

1

Saw ye my Maggie?
Saw ye my Maggie?
Saw ye my Maggie?
  Comin oer the lea?

2

What mark has your Maggie,
What mark has your Maggie,
What mark has your Maggie,
  That ane may ken her be?

[2a]

[Wry-c—d is she,
 Wry-c—d is she,
 Wry-c—d is she,
  And pishes gain' her thie.]

3

My Maggie has a mark,
Ye'll find it in the dark,
It's in below her sark,
  A little aboon her knee.

4

What wealth has your Maggie,
What wealth has your Maggie,
What wealth has your Maggie,
  In tocher, gear, or fee?

5

My Maggie has a treasure,
A hidden mine o' pleasure,
I'll howk it at my leisure,
   It's alane for me.

6

How loe ye your Maggy,
How loe [ye] your Maggy,
How loe ye your Maggy,
   An loe nane but she?

7

Ein that tell our wishes,
Eager glowing kisses,
Then diviner blisses,
   In holy ecstacy!—

8

How meet you your Maggie,
How meet you your Maggie,
How meet you your Maggie,
   When nane's to hear or see?

9

Heavenly joys before me,
Rapture trembling o'er me,
Maggie I adore thee,
   On my bended knee!!!

TO ALEXANDER FINDLATER

❦

Ellisland Saturday morning.

Dear Sir,

    our Lucky humbly begs
Ye'll prie her caller, new-laid eggs:
L—d grant the Cock may keep his legs,
    Aboon the Chuckies;
And wi' his kittle, forket clegs,
    Claw weel their dockies!

Had Fate that curst me in her ledger,
A Poet poor, & poorer Gager,
Created me that feather'd Sodger,
    A generous Cock,
How I wad craw & strut and r—ger
    My kecklin Flock!

Buskit wi' mony a bien, braw feather,
I wad defied the warst o' weather:
When corn or bear I could na gather
    To gie my burdies;
I'd treated them wi' caller heather,
    And weel-knooz'd hurdies.

Nae cursed CLERICAL EXCISE
On honest Nature's laws & ties;
Free as the vernal breeze that flies
    At early day,
We'd tasted Nature's richest joys,
    But stint or stay.—

But as this subject's something kittle,
Our wisest way's to say but little;
And while my Muse is at her mettle,
      I am, most fervent,
Or may I die upon a whittle!
      Your Friend & Servant—

ROBt BURNS

THE FORNICATOR

TUNE: *Clout the Cauldron*

ᴏ◈ᴏ

A new Song

Ye jovial boys who love the joys,
   The blissful joys of Lovers,
Yet dare avow, with dauntless brow,
   When the bony lass discovers,
I pray draw near, and lend an ear,
   And welcome in a Frater,
For I've lately been on quarantine,
   A proven Fornicator.

Before the Congregation wide,
   I passed the muster fairly,
My handsome Betsy by my side,
   We gat our ditty rarely;
But my downcast eye did chance to spy
   What made my lips to water,
Those limbs so clean where I between
   Commenc'd a Fornicator.

With rueful face and signs of grace
   I pay'd the buttock-hire,
But the night was dark and thro' the park
   I could not but convoy her;
A parting kiss, I could not less,
   My vows began to scatter,
My Betsy fell—lal de dal lal lal,
   I am a Fornicator.

But for her sake this vow I make,
    And solemnly I swear it,
That while I own a single crown
    She's welcome for to share it;
And my roguish boy his Mother's joy
    And the darling of his Pater,
For him I boast my pains and cost,
    Although a Fornicator.

Ye wenching blades whose hireling jades
    Have tipt you off blue-joram,
I tell you plain, I do disdain
    To rank you in the Quorum;
But a bony lass upon the grass
    To teach her esse Mater,
And no reward but fond regard,
    O that's a Fornicator.

Your warlike Kings and Heros bold,
    Great Captains and Commanders;
Your mighty Caesars fam'd of old,
    And conquering Alexanders;
In fields they fought and laurels bought,
    And bulwarks strong did batter,
But still they grac'd our noble list,
    And ranked Fornicator!!!

MY GIRL SHE'S AIRY

TUNE: *Black Joke*

❦

My Girl she's airy, she's buxom and gay,
Her breath is as sweet as the blossoms in May;
   A touch of her lips it ravishes quite;
She's always good natur'd, good humor'd and free;
She dances, she glances, she smiles with a glee;
   Her eyes are the lightenings of joy and delight;
Her slender neck, her handsome waist
Her hair well buckl'd, her stays well lac'd,
Her taper white leg, with an et, and a, c,
    For her a, b, e, d, and her c, u, n, t,
    And Oh, for the joys of a long winter night!!!

THERE WAS TWA WIVES

✧

There was twa wives, and twa witty wives,
  As e'er play'd houghmagandie,
And they coost out, upon a time,
  Out o'er a drink o' brandy;
Up Maggy rose, and forth she goes,
  And she leaves auld Mary flytin,
And she f—rted by the byre-en'
  For she was gaun a sh—ten.

She f—rted by the byre-en'
  She f—rted by the stable;
And thick and nimble were her steps
  As fast as she was able:
Till at yon dyke-back the hurly brak,
  But raxin for some dockins,
The beans and pease eam down her thighs,
  And she cackit a' her stockins.

B. *Collected by Burns*

BROSE AN' BUTTER

Gie my Love brose, brose,
  Gie my Love brose an' butter;
An' gie my Love brose, brose,
  Yestreen he wanted his supper.

Jenny sits up i' the laft,
  Jocky wad fain a been at her;
There cam a win' out o' the wast
  Made a' the windows to clatter.
      Gie my Love brose &c.

A dow's a dainty dish;
  A goose is hollow within;
A sight wad mak you blush,
  But a' the fun's to fin'.
      Gie my &c.

My Dadie sent me to the hill,
  To pow my minnie some heather;
An' drive it in your fill,
  Ye're welcome to the leather.
      Gie my &c.

A mouse is a merry wee beast;
  A modewurck wants the een;
An' O for the touch o' the thing
  I had i' my nieve yestreen.
      Gie my Love &c.

The lark she loves the grass;
   The hen she loves the stibble;
An' hey for the Gar'ner lad,
   To gully awa wi' his dibble.—

As I looked o'er yon castle wa',
  I spied a grey goose & a gled;
They had a fecht between them twa,
  And O, as their twa hurdies gade.—

Chorus

  With a hey ding it in, & a how ding it in,
    And a hey ding it in, it's lang to day:
  Tal larietal, tallarietal
    Tal larietal, tal larie tay.

2

She strack up & he strack down.
  Between them twa they made a mowe,
And ilka fart that the carlin gae,
  It's four o' them wad fill a bowe.
                    With a hey ding it in &c.

3

Temper your tail, Carlin, he cried,
  Temper your tail by Venus' law;
Double your dunts, the dame replied,
  Wha the deil can hinder the wind to blaw!
                    With a hey &c.

4

For were ye in my saddle set,
  And were ye weel girt in my gear,
If the wind o' my arse blaw you out o' my cunt,
  Ye'll never be reckoned a man o' weir.—
                    With a hey &c.

He placed his Jacob whare she did piss,
   And his ballocks whare the wind did blaw,
And he grippet her fast by the goosset o' the arse
   And he gae her cunt the common law.
            With a hey &c.

GREEN GROW THE RASHES O (A)

❧❦❧

A Fragment—

Chorus

Green grow the rashes O,
Green grow the rashes O,
The lasses they hae wimble bores,
The widows they hae gashes O.

1

In sober hours I am a priest;
  A hero when I'm tipsey, O;
But I'm a king and ev'ry thing,
  When wi' a wanton Gipsey, O.

Green grow &c.

2

'Twas late yestreen I met wi' ane,
  An' wow, but she was gentle, O!
Ae han' she pat roun' my cravat,
  The tither to my p—— O.

Green grow &c.

3

I dought na speak—yet was na fley'd—
  My heart play'd duntie, duntie, O;
An' ceremony laid aside,
  I fairly fun' her c—ntie, O.—
      Green grow &c.

—*Multa desunt*—

MUIRLAND MEG

TUNE: *Saw ye my Eppie McNab?*

◦◈◦

Among our young lassies there's Muirland Meg,
She'll beg or she work, & she'll play or she beg,
At thirteen her maidenhead flew to the gate,
And the door o' her cage stands open yet.—

Her kittle black een they wad thirl you thro'.
Her rose-bud lips cry, kiss me now;
The curls & links o' her bonie black hair,—
Wad put you in mind that the lassie has mair.—

An armfu' o' love is her bosom sae plump,
A span o' delight is her middle sae jimp;
A taper, white leg, & a thumpin thie,
And a fiddle near by, an ye play a wee!—

Love's her delight, & kissin's her treasure;
She'll stick at nae price, & ye gie her gude measure,
As lang's a sheep-fit, & as girt's a goose-egg,
And that's the measure o' Muirland Meg.

TODLEN HAME

(By David McCulloch of Ardwell, Galloway)

꘎꘎꘎

When wise Solomon was a young man o' might,
He was canty, & liked a lass ilka night;
But when he grew auld that he was na in trim,
He cried out, "In faith, Sirs! I doubt it's a sin!"

    Todlen hame, todlen hame,
    Sae round as a neep we gang todlen hame.—

But we're no come to that time o' life yet, ye ken;
The bottle's half-out—but we'll fill it again:
As for Solomon's doubts, wha the devil cares for't!
He's a damn'd churlish fallow that likes to spill sport.

    Todlen &c.

A bicker that's gizzen'd, it's nae worth a doit;
Keep it wat, it will haud in—it winna let out:
A chiel that's ay sober, is damn'd ill to ken;
Keep him wat wi' gude drink—& ye'll find him out
    then.—

    Todlen &c.

May our house be weel theekit, our pantry ay fu',
Wi' rowth in our cellar for weetin' our mou';
Wi a tight, caller hizzie, as keen as oursels,
Ay ready to souple *the whistle & bells!!!*

    Todlen hame &c.

WAP AND ROW

⚬✧⚬

Chorus—(Note, the song begins with the Chorus)

> Wap & row, wap & row,
>> Wap & row the feetie o't
> I thought I was a maiden fair,
>> Till I heard the greetie o't.—

> My daddie was a fiddler fine,
>> My minnie she made mantie, O,
> And I myself a thumpin quine,
>> And try'd the rantie-tantie O.

> Wap and row &c.

THERE CAM A SOGER

There cam a soger here to stay,
    He swore he wadna steer me;
But, lang before the break o' day,
    He cuddl'd muddl'd near me:
He set a stiff thing to my wame,
    I docht na bide the bends o't;
But lang before the grey morn cam,
    I soupl'd baith the ends o't.—

SING, UP WI'T, AILY

Sing, Up wi't, Aily, Aily;
  Down wi' kimmerland jock;
Deil ram their lugs, quo' Willie,
  But I hae scour'd her dock!

Encore!

GREEN SLEEVES

❁

Green sleeves and tartan ties
Mark my true love whare she lies:
I'll be at her or she rise,
   My fiddle and I thegither.

Be it by the chrystal burn,
Be it by the milkwhite thorn;
I shall rouse her in the morn,
   My fiddle and I thegither.

Another version reads:

Green sleeves and pudden-pyes,
Come tell me where my true love lyes,
And I'll be wi' her ere she rise:
   Fidle a' the gither!

Hey ho! and about she goes,
She's milk in her breasts, she's none in her toes,
She's a hole in her a—, you may put in your nose,
   Sing: hey, boys, up go we!

Green sleeves and yellow lace,
Maids, maids, come, marry a pace!
The batchelors are in a pitiful case
   To fidle a' the gither.

                      [SGS]

II

❧

BY OR
ATTRIBUTED
TO BURNS
FROM PRINTED SOURCES

THE PATRIARCH

TUNE (in MMC): *The Auld Cripple Dow*

As honest Jacob on a night,
  Wi' his beloved beauty,
Was duly laid on wedlock's bed,
  And noddin' at his duty.
                Tal de dal &c.

"How lang, she says, ye fumblin' wretch,
  "Will ye be f—g at it?
"My eldest wean might die of age,
  "Before that ye could get it.

"Ye pegh and grane, and groazle there,
  "And mak an unco splutter,
"And I maun ly and thole you here,
  "And fient a hair the better."

Then he, in wrath, put up his graith,
  "The deevil's in the hizzie!
"I m—w you as I m—w the lave,
  "And night and day I'm bisy.

"I've bairn'd the servant gypsies baith,
  "Forbye your titty Leah;
"Ye barren jad, ye put me mad,
  "What mair can I do wi you.

"There's ne'er a m—w I've gi'en the lave,
  "But ye ha'e got a dizzen;
"An d—n'd a ane ye'se get again,
  "Although your c—t should gizzen."

Then Rachel calm, as ony lamb,
   She claps him on the waulies;
Quo' she, "ne'er fash a woman's clash,
   "In trowth ye m—w me braulies.

"My dear 'tis true, for mony a m—w,
   "I'm your ungratefu' debtor,
"But ance again, I dinna ken,
   "We'll aiblens happen better."

Then honest man! wi' little wark,
   He soon forgat his ire;
The patriarch, he coost the sark,
   And up and till't like fire!

THE BONNIEST LASS

The bonniest lass that ye meet neist
   Gie her a kiss an' a' that,
In spite o' ilka parish priest,
   Repentin' stool, an' a' that.

     For a' that an' a' that,
       Their mim-mou'd sangs an' a' that,
     In time and place convenient,
       They'll do't themselves for a' that.

Your patriarchs in days o' yore,
   Had their handmaids an' a' that;
O' bastard gets, some had a score
   An' some had mair than a' that.

     For a' that an' a' that,
       Your langsyne saunts, an' a' that,
     Were fonder o' a bonie lass,
       Than you or I, for a' that.

King Davie, when he waxed auld,
   An's bluid ran thin, an' a' that,
An' fand his cods were growin' cauld,
   Could not refrain, for a' that.

     For a' that an' a' that,
       To keep him warm an' a' that,
     The daughters o' Jerusalem
       Were waled for him, an' a' that.

Wha wadna pity thae sweet dames
   He fumbled at, an' a' that,

An' raised their bluid up into flames
   He couldna drown, for a' that.

     For a' that an' a' that,
       He wanted pith, an' a' that;
     For, as to what we shall not name,
       What could he do but claw that.

King Solomon, prince o' divines,
   Wha proverbs made, an' a' that,
Baith mistresses an' concubines
   In hundreds had, for a' that.

     For a' that an' a' that,
       Tho' a preacher wise an' a' that,
     The smuttiest sang that e'er was sung
       His Sang o' Sangs is a' that.

Then still I swear, a clever chiel
   Should kiss a lass, an' a' that,
Tho' priests consign him to the deil,
   As reprobate, an' a' that.

     For a' that an' a' that,
       Their canting stuff, an' a' that,
     They ken nae mair wha's reprobate
       Than you or I, for a' that.

GODLY GIRZIE

TUNE: *Wat ye wha I met yestreen?*

◦❖◦

The night it was a haly night,
    The day had been a haly day;
Kilmarnock gleamed wi' candle light,
    As Girzie hameward took her way.
A man o' sin, ill may he thrive!
    And never haly-meeting see!
Wi' godly Girzie met belyve,
    Amang the Cragie hills sae hie.

The chiel' was wight, the chiel' was stark,
    He wad na wait to chap nor ca',
And she was faint wi haly wark,
    She had na pith to say him na.
But ay she glowr'd up to the moon,
    And ay she sigh'd most piouslie;
"I trust my heart's in heaven aboon,
    "Whare'er your sinfu' p—e be."

WHA'LL MOW ME NOW?

TUNE: *Comin' thro' the rye*

⌒⟡⌒

O, I hae tint my rosy cheek,
    Likewise my waste sae sma';
O wae gae by the sodger lown,
    The sodger did it a'.

    O wha'll m—w me now, my jo,
        An' wha'll m—w me now:
    A sodger wi' his bandileers
        Has bang'd my belly fu'.

Now I maun thole the scornfu' sneer
    O' mony a saucy quine;
When, curse upon her godly face!
    Her c—t's as merry's mine.

Our dame hauds up her wanton tail,
    As due as she gaes lie;
An' yet misca's [a] young thing,
    The trade if she but try.

Our dame can lae her ain gudeman,
    An' m—w for glutton greed;
An' yet misca' a poor thing,
    That's m—n' for its bread.

Alake! sae sweet a tree as love,
    Sic bitter fruit should bear!
Alake, that e'er a merry a—e,
    Should draw a sa'tty tear.

But deevil damn the lousy loon,
    Denies the bairn he got!
Or lea's the merry a—e he lo'ed,
    To wear a ragged coat!

HAD I THE WYTE SHE BADE ME (A)

TUNE: *Highland Hills*

Had I the wyte, had I the wyte,
  Had I the wyte she bad me;
For she was steward in the house,
  And I was fit-man laddie;
And when I wadna do't again,
  A silly cow * she ca'd me;
She straik't my head, and clapt my cheeks,
  And lous'd my breeks and bad me.

Could I for shame, could I for shame,
  Could I for shame deny['d] her;
Or in the bed was I to blame,
  She bad me lye beside her:
I pat six inches in her wame,
  A quarter wadna fly'd her;
For ay the mair I ca'd it hame,
  Her ports they grew the wider.

My tartan plaid, when it was dark,
  Could I refuse to share it;
She lifted up her holland-sark,
  And bad me fin' the gair o't:
Or how could I amang the garse,
  But gie her hilt and hair o't;
She clasped her houghs about my a—e,
  And ay she glowr'd for mair o't.

DAINTY DAVIE (A)

❧❧❧

Being pursu'd by the dragoons,
   Within my bed he was laid down
And weel I wat he was worth his room,
   My ain dear dainty Davie.

     O leeze me on * his curly pow,
     Bonie Davie, dainty Davie;
     Leeze me on his curly pow,
     He was my dainty Davie.

My minnie laid him at my back,
   I trow he lay na lang at that,
But turn'd, and in a verra crack
   Produc'd a dainty Davie.

Then in the field amang the pease,
   Behin' the house o' Cherrytrees,
Again he wan atweesh my thies,
   And, splash! gaed out his gravy.

But had I goud, or had I land,
   It should be a' at his command;
I'll ne'er forget what he pat i' my hand,
   It was a dainty Davie.

*See footnote, p. 10

[41]

THE TROGGER

TUNE: *Gillicrankie*

As I cam down by Annan side,
  Intending for the border,
Amang the Scroggie banks and braes
  Wha met I but a trogger.
He laid me down upon my back,
  I thought he was but jokin',
Till he was in me to the hilts,
  O the deevil tak sic troggin!

What could I say, what could I do,
  I bann'd and sair misca'd him,
But whiltie-whaltie gaed his a—e,
  The mair that I forbade him:
He stell'd his foot against a stane,
  And double'd ilka stroke in,
Till I gaed daft amang his hands,
  O the deevil tak sic troggin!

Then up we raise, and took the road,
  And in by Ecclefechan,
Where the brandy-stoup we gart it clink,
  And the strang-beer ream the quech in.
Bedown the bents o' Bonshaw braes,
  We took the partin' yokin';
But I've claw'd a sairy c—t sinsyne,
  O the deevil tak sic troggin!

PUT BUTTER IN MY DONALD'S BROSE

◦◈◦

Put butter in my Donald's brose,
  For weel does Donald fa' that;
I loe my Donald's tartans weel
  His naked a—e and a' that.

    For a' that, and a' that,
      And twice as meikle's a' that,
    The lassie gat a skelpit doup,
      But wan the day for a' that.

For Donald swore a solemn aith,
  By his first hairy gravat!
That he wad fight the battle there,
  And stick the lass, and a' that.

His hairy b—s, side and wide,
  Hang like a beggar's wallet;
A p—e like a roaring-pin,
  She nicher'd when she saw that!!!

Then she turn'd up her hairy c—t,
  And she bade Donald claw that;
The deevil's dizzen Donald drew,
  And Donald gied her a' that.

TUNE: *The job o' journey wark* (says SD)

❧

Altho' my back be at the wa,
    An' tho' he be the fau'tor;
Altho' my back be at the wa',
    I'll drink his health in water.
O wae gae by his wanton sides,
    Sae brawly's he cou'd flatter.
I for his sake am slighted sair,
    An' dree the kintra clatter;
But let them say whate'er they like,
    Yet, here's his health in water.

He follow'd me baith out an' in,
    Thro' a' the nooks o' Killie;
He follow'd me baith out an' in,
    Wi' a stiff stanin' p-llie.
But when he gat atween my legs,
    We made an unco splatter;
An' haith, I trow, I soupled it,
    Tho' bauldly he did blatter;
But now my back is at the wa',
    Yet here's his health in water.

THE JOLLY GAUGER

TUNE: *We'll gang nae mair a rovin'*

◦◈◦

There was a jolly gauger, a gauging he did ride,
And he has met a beggar down by yon river side.

  An weel gang nae mair a rovin' wi' ladies to the wine,
  When a beggar wi' her meal-pocks can fidge her tail
    sae fine.

Amang the broom he laid her; amang the broom sae
    green,
And he's fa'n to the beggar, as she had been a queen.

  And we'll gang &c.

My blessings on thee, laddie, thou's done my turn sae
    weel,
Wilt thou accept, dear laddie, my pock and pickle
    meal?

  And weel, &c.

Sae blyth the beggar took the bent, like ony bird in
    spring,
Sae blyth the beggar took the bent, and merrily did
    sing.

  And weel, &c.

My blessings on the gauger, o' gaugers he's the chief,
Sic kail ne'er crost my kettle, nor sic a joint o'beef.

  And weel, &c.

O GAT YE ME WI NAETHING?

TUNE: *Jacky Latin*

❧❖❧

Gat ye me, O gat ye me,
   An' gat ye me wi' naething?
A rock, a reel, a spinning wheel,
   A gude black c—t was ae thing.
A tocher fine, o'er muckle far,
   When sic a scullion gat it;
Indeed, o'er muckle far, gudewife,
   For that was ay the fau't o't.

But had your tongue now, Luckie Lang,
   O had your tongue and jander,
I held the gate till you I met,
   Syne I began to wander;
I tint my whistle an' my sang,
   I tint my peace an' pleasure,
But your green grave now, Luckie Lang,
   Wad airt me to my treasure.

GIE THE LASS HER FAIRIN'

TUNE: *Cauld kail in Aberdeen*

O gie the lass her fairin' lad,
  O gie the lass her fairin',
An' something else she'll gie to you,
  That's waly worth the wearin';
Syne coup her o'er amang the creels,
  When ye hae taen your brandy,
The mair she bangs the less she squeels,
  An' hey for houghmagandie.

Then gie the lass a fairin', lad,
  O gie the lass her fairin',
And she'll gie you a hairy thing,
  An' of it be na sparin';
But coup her o'er amang the creels,
  An' bar the door wi' baith your heels,
The mair she bangs the less she squeels,
  An' hey for houghmagandie.

GREEN GROW THE RASHES (B)

O wat ye ought o' fisher Meg,
    And how she trow'd the webster, O,
She loot me see her carrot c—t,
    And sell'd it for a labster, O.

        Green grow the rashes, O,
            Green grow the rashes, O,
        The lassies they hae wimble-bores,
            The widows they hae gashes, O.

Mistress Mary cow'd her thing,
    Because she wad be gentle, O,
And span the fleece upon a rock,
    To waft a Highland mantle, O.

An' heard ye o' the coat o' arms,
    The Lyon brought our lady, O,
The crest was, couchant, sable c—t,
    The motto—"*ready, ready,*" O.

An' ken ye Leezie Lundie, O.
    The godly Leezie Lundie, O,
She m—s like reek thro' a' the week,
    But finger f—s on Sunday, O.

TAIL TODLE

TUNE: *Chevalier's Muster-Roll* (says SD)

❧

Our gudewife held o'er to Fife,
　For to buy a coal-riddle;
Lang or she came back again,
　Tammie gart my tail todle.

　　Tail todle, tail todle;
　　Tammie gart my tail todle;
　　At my a—e wi' diddle doddle,
　　Tammie gart my tail todle.

When I'm dead I'm out o' date;
　When I'm sick I'm fu' o' trouble;
When I'm weel I step about,
　An' Tammie gars my tail todle.

Jenny Jack she gae a plack,
　Helen Wallace gae a boddle,
Quo' the bride, it's o'er little
　For to mend a broken doddle.

I REDE YOU BEWARE O' THE RIPPLES

TUNE: *The Taylor's faun thro the bed*

◦❖◦

I rede you beware o' the ripples, young man,
I rede you beware o' the ripples, young man;
Tho' the saddle be saft, ye needna ride aft,
For fear that the girdin' beguile ye, young man.

I rede you beware o' the ripples, young man,
I rede you beware o' the ripples, young man;
Tho' music be pleasure, tak' music in measure,
Or ye may want win' i' your whistle, young man.

I rede you beware o' the ripples, young man,
I rede you beware o' the ripples, young man;
Whate'er ye bestow, do less than ye dow,
The mair will be thought o' your kindness, young man.

I rede you beware o' the ripples, young man,
I rede you beware o' the ripples, young man;
Gif you wad be strang, and wish to live lang,
Dance less wi' your a—e to the kipples, young man.

OUR JOHN'S BRAK YESTREEN

TUNE: *Gramachree*

Twa neebor wives sat i' the sun,
   A twynin' at their rocks,
An' they an argument began,
   An' a' the plea was c—ks.

'Twas whether they were sinnens strang,
   Or whether they were bane?
An' how they row'd about your thumb,
   And how they stan't themlane?

First, Raichie gae her rock a rug,
   An' syne she claw'd her tail;
"When our Tam draws on his breeks,
   "It waigles like a flail."

Says Bess, "they're bane I will maintain,
   "And proof in han' I'll gie;
"For our John's it brak yestreen,
   "And the margh ran down my thie."

GRIZZEL GRIMME

Grim Grizzel was a mighty Dame
   Weel kend on Cluden-side:
Grim Grizzel was a mighty Dame
   O' meikle fame and pride.

When gentles met in gentle bowers
   And nobles in the ha',
Grim Grizzle was a mighty Dame,
   The loudest o' them a'.

Where lawless Riot rag'd the night
   And Beauty durst na gang,
Grim Grizzel was a mighty Dame
   Wham nae man e'er wad wrang.

Nor had Grim Grizzel skill alane
   What bower and ha' require;
But she had skill, and meikle skill,
   In barn and eke in byre.

Ae day Grim Grizzel walkèd forth,
   As she was wont to do,
Alang the banks o' Cluden fair,
   Her cattle for to view.

The cattle sh— o'er hill and dale
   As cattle will incline,
And sair it grieved Grim Grizzel's heart
   Sae muckle muck tae tine.

And she has ca'd on John o' Clods,
   Of her herdsmén the chief,
And she has ca'd on John o' Clods,
   And tell'd him a' her grief:—

"Now wae betide thee, John o' Clods!
  I gie thee meal and fee,
And yet sae meickle muck ye tine
  Might a' be gear to me!

"Ye claut my byre, ye sweep my byre,
  The like was never seen;
The very chamber I lie in
  Was never half sae clean.

"Ye ca' my kye adown the loan
  And there they a' discharge:
My Tammie's hat, wig, head and a'
  Was never half sae large!

"But mind my words now, John o' Clods,
  And tent me what I say:
My kye shall sh— ere they gae out,
  That shall they ilka day.

"And mind my words now, John o' Clods,
  And tent now wha ye serve;
Or back ye'se to the Colonel gang,
  Either to steal or starve."

Then John o' Clods, he lookèd up
  And syne he lookèd down;
He lookèd east, he lookèd west,
  He lookèd roun' and roun'.

His bonnet and his rowantree club
  Frae either hand did fa';
Wi' lifted een and open mouth
  He naething said at a'.

At length he found his trembling tongue,
    Within his mouth was fauld:—
"Ae silly word frae me, madám,
    Gin I daur be sae bauld.

"Your kye will at nae bidding sh—,
    Let me do what I can;
Your kye will at nae bidding sh—,
    Of onie earthly man.

"Tho' ye are great Lady Glaur-hole,
    For a' your power and art
Tho' ye are great Lady Glaur-hole,
    They winna let a fart."

"Now wae betide thee, John o' Clods!
    An ill death may ye die!
My kye shall at my bidding sh—,
    And that ye soon shall see."

Then she's ta'en Hawkie by the tail,
    And wrung wi' might and main,
Till Hawkie rowted through the woods
    Wi' agonising pain.

"Sh—, sh—, ye bitch," Grim Grizzel roar'd,
    Till hill and valley rang;
"And sh—, ye bitch," the echoes roar'd
    Lincluden wa's amang.

TWO EPITAPHS

❦

❦

Lament him, M[auchline] husbands a',
   He aften did assist ye!
Tho ye had bidden years awa
   Your wives [wad] ne'er hae miss't ye.

Ye M[auchline] bairns, as bye ye pass
   To school in bands thegither,
O tread but lightly on the grass,
   Perhaps he was your father!

EPITAPH FOR
H[UGH] L[OGAN], ESQ., OF L[AIGHT]

❦

Here lyes Squire Hugh—ye harlot crew,
   Come mak' your water on him,
I'm sure that he weel pleas'd would be
   To think ye pish'd upon him.

III

❖

OLD SONGS
USED BY BURNS
FOR
POLITE VERSIONS

HAD I THE WYTE? (B)

Had I the wyte? had I the wyte?
Had I the wyte? She bad me,
And ay she gied me cheese and bread
To kiss her when she bad me,
For she was stewart in the house,
And I was footman-ladie,
And ay she gied me cheese and bread
To kiss her, when she bad me.

DAINTY DAVIE (B)

It was in and through the window broads,
And all the tirliewirlies o'd:
The sweetest kiss that e'er I got
Was from my Dainty Davie.

O leeze me on * your curly pow,
Dainty Davie, dainty Davie,
Leeze me on your curly pow,
Mine ain dainty Davie.

It was down amang my daddy's pease,
And underneath the cherry-trees:
O there he kist me as he pleas'd,
For he was mine ain dear Davie.

When he was chased by a dragoon,
Into my bed he was laid down,
I thought him wordy o' his room,
And he's ay my dainty Davie.

* See footnote, p. 58.

*See footnote, p. 10

LET ME IN THIS AE NIGHT

O lassie, art thou sleeping yet,
Or are you waking, I wou'd wit?
For love has bound me hand and foot,
And I woul'd fain be in, jo.

O let me in this ae night, this ae, ae, ae night,
O let me in this ae night, and I'll ne'er come back
again, jo.

The morn it is the term-day,
I maun away, I canna stay:
O pity me, before I gae,
And rise and let me in, jo.

O let me in this ae night, this ae, ae, ae night,
O let me in this ae night, and I'll ne'er come back
again, jo.

The night it is baith cauld and weet,
The morn it will be snaw and sleet,
My shoen are frozen to my feet
Wi' standing on the plain, jo.

O let me in this ae night, this ae, ae, ae night,
O let me in this ae night, and I'll ne'er come back
again, jo.

I am the laird of windy-was,
I come na here without a cause,

And I hae gotten mony fa's
Upon a naked wame o!

O let me in this ae night, this ae, ae, ae night,
O let me in this ae night, and I'll ne'er come back
again, jo.

My father's wa'king on the street,
My mither the chamber-keys does keep,
My chamber-door does chirp and cheep,
And I dare nae let you in, jo!

O gae your way this ae night, this ae, ae, ae night
O gae your way this ae night, for I dare nae let you
in, jo!

But I'll come stealing saftly in
And cannily make little dinn,
And then the gate to you I'll find,
If you'l but direct me in, jo!

O let me in this ae night, this ae, ae, ae night,
O let me in this ae night, and I'll ne'er come back
again, jo.

Cast aff the shoen frae aff your feet,
Cast back the door up to the weet,
Syne into my bed you may creep
And do the thing you ken, jo.

O well's on me this ae night, this ae, ae, ae night,
O well's on me this ae night, that ere I let you in, jo!

She let him in sae cannily,
She let him in sae privily,
She let him in sae cannily,
To do the thing ye ken, jo.

O well's on me this ae night, this ae, ae, ae night,
O well's on me this ae night, that ere I let you in, jo!

But ere a' was done and a' was said,
Out fell the bottom of the bed,
The lassie lost her maidenhead,
And her mither heard the din, jo.

O the devil take this ae night, this ae, ae, ae night,
O the devil take this ae night, that ere I let ye in, jo!

THE TAILOR

The tailor came to clout the claise,
    Sic a braw fellow,
He filled the house a' fou o' fleas,
    Daffin down, and daffin down,
He filled the house a 'fou o' fleas,
    Daffin down and dilly.

The lassie slept ayont the fire,
    Sic a braw hissey!
Oh! she was a' his heart's desire,
    Daffin down, and daffin down,
Oh! she was a' his heart's desire,
    Daffin down and dilly.

The lassie she fell fast asleep,
    Sic a braw hissey!
The tailor close to her did creep,
    Daffin down, and daffin down,
The tailor close to her did creep,
    Daffin down and dilly.

The lassie waken'd in a fright,
    Sic a braw hissey!
Her maidenhead had taen the flight,
    Daffin down, and daffin down,
A tailor's bodkin caused the flight,
    Daffin down and dilly.

She sought it butt, she sought it ben,
   Sic a braw hissey!
And in beneath the clocken-hen,
   Daffin down, and daffin down,
It wasna but, it wasna ben,
   Daffin down and dilly.

She sought it in the owsen-staw,
   Sic a braw hissey!
Na, faith, quo' she, it's quite awa',
   Daffin down, and daffin down,
The tailor loon has stown't awa',
   Daffin down and dilly.

She sought it 'yont the knocking-stane,
   Sic a braw hissey!
Some day, quo' she, 'twill gang its lane,
   Daffin down, and daffin down,
For my tirly-wirly mak's its mane,
   Daffin down and dilly.

She ca'd the tailor to the court,
   Sic a braw hissey!
And a' the young men round about,
   Daffin down, and daffin down,
To gar the tailor mend her clout,
   Daffin down and dilly.

She gart the tailor pay a fine,
   Sic a braw hissey!
Gi'e me my maidenhead agen;
   Daffin down, and daffin down,
I'll hae my maidenhead again,
   Daffin down and dilly.

O what way wad ye hae't agen?
  Sic a braw hissey!
Oh! just the way that it was taen,
  Daffin down, and daffin down,
Come, just the way that it was ta'en,
  Daffin down and dilly.

EPPIE McNAB

O saw ye my Eppie McNab, McNab?
O saw ye my Eppie McNab, McNab?
She's down i' the yeard, she's kissen the laird,
As whilom's wi' honest Jock Rob, Jock Rob.

My blessings upo' thee, Jock Rob, Jock Rob,
My blessings upo' thee, Jock Rob, Jock Rob,
For in my gavel ye drive sic a dool,
Gard a' my buttocks play bab, bab, bab.

When first I met wi' thee, Jock Rob, Jock Rob,
When first I met wi' thee, Jock Rob, Jock Rob!
Thy breeks they were hol'd, and thy — hung out,
And thy — play'd ay did dod, did dod.

When first I met Eppie McNab, McNab,
I met wi' Eppie McNab, McNab;
Thy wee bit dud sark it play'd dod o' thy dab,
And thy — was as black as a crab, a crab.

DUNCAN GRAY

Can ye play me Duncan Gray,
  Ha, ha, the girdin' o't;
O'er the hills an' far awa,
  Ha, ha, ha, the girdin' o't,
Duncan came our Meg to woo,
Meg was nice an' wadna do,
But like an ither puff'd an' blew
  At offer o' the girdin' o't.

Duncan, he cam here again,
  Ha, ha, the girdin' o't,
A' was out, an' Meg her lane,
  Ha, ha, ha, the girdin' o't;
He kiss'd her butt, he kiss'd her ben,
He bang'd a thing against her wame;
But, troth, I now forget its name,
  But, I trow, she gat the girdin' o't.

She took him to the cellar then,
  Ha, ha, the girdin' o't,
To see gif he could do't again,
  Ha, ha, ha, the girdin' o't;
He kiss'd her ance, he kiss'd her twice,
An' by the bye he kiss'd her thrice
Till deil a mair the thing wad rise
  To gie her the long girdin' o't.

But Duncan took her to his wife,
  Ha, ha, the girdin' o't,
To be the comfort o' his life,

Ha, ha, ha, the girdin' o't;
An' now she scauls baith night an' day,
Except when Duncan's at the play;
An' that's as seldom as he may,
He's weary o'the girdin' o't.

LOGAN WATER

The Logan burn, the Logan braes,
I helped a bonie lassie on wi' her claes;
First wi' her stockings an' syne wi' her shoon,
But she gied me the glaiks when a' was done.

But an I had kend, what I ken now,
I wad a bang'd her belly fu';
Her belly fu' and her apron up,
An' shew'd her the road to the Logan kirk.

THE MILL MILL-O

As I came down yon water side
  And by yon Shillin hill, O;
There I spied a bonny lass,
  A lass that I loed right weel, O.

> The mill, mill, O, and the kill, kill, O,
> An' the coggin' o' Peggy's wheel, O,
> The sack an' the sieve, a' she did leave,
> An' danc'd the millars reel, O.

I spier'd at her, gin she cou'd play,
  But the lassie had nae skill, O;
An' yet she was nae a' to blame,
  She pat it in my will, O.

Then she fell o'er, an' sae did I,
  And danc'd the millars reel, O,
Whene'er that bonny lassie comes again,
  She shall hae her ma't ground weel, O.

MY AIN KIND DEARIE

TUNE: *The Lea Rig*

❦

I'll lay thee o'er the lee-rig,
  Lovely Mary, deary, O;
I'll lay thee o'er the lee-rig,
  My lovely Mary, deary, O.
Altho' the night were ne'er so wet,
  An' I were ne'er so weary O;
I'd lay thee o'er the lee-rig,
  My lovely Mary, deary, O.

Look down ye gods from yonder sky,
  An' see how blest a man am I;
No envy my fond heart alarms,
  Encircled in my Mary's arms.
Lyin' across the lee-rig,
  Wi' lovely Mary, deary, O;
Lyin' across the lee-rig,
  Wi' my ain kind deary, O.

SHE ROSE AND LOOT ME IN

The night her silent sable wore,
   An' gloomin' was the skies;
O' glitt'rin' stars appear'd no more
   Than those in Nelly's eyes:
When at her father's gate I knock'd,
   Where I had often been;
Shrouded only in her smock,
   She rose an' loot me in.

Fast lock'd within my fond embrace,
   She tremblin' stood asham'd;
Her glowin' lips an' heavin' breasts,
   At every touch enflam'd;
My eager passion I obey'd,
   Resolv'd the fort to win;
An' she, at last, gave her consent
   To yeild an' let me in.

O then! what bliss beyond compare,
   I knew no greater joy;
Enroll'd in heavenly happiness,
   So bless'd a man was I;
An' she, all ravish'd with delight,
   Bad me aft come again,
An' kindly vow'd that ev'ry night
   She'd rise an' let me in.

But ah! at last, she prov'd wi' bairn,
   An' sat baith sad an' dull;
An' I wha was as much concern'd,

Look'd e'en just like a fool;
Her lovely eyes wi' tears ran o'er,
    Repentin' her rash sin;
An' ay she curs'd the fatal hour
    That e'er she loot me in.

But, who cou'd from such beauty go,
    Or yet from Nelly part;
I lov'd her dear, an' couldna leave
    The charmer of my heart,
We wedded and conceal'd our crime,
    Then all was weel again,
An' now she blesses the happy night
    She rose an' loot me in.

THE COOPER O' DUNDEE

TUNE: *Bonny Dundee*

◦❖◦

Ye coopers and hoopers attend to my ditty,
    I sing o' a cooper who dwelt in Dundee;
This young man he was baith am'rous and witty,
    He pleas'd the fair maids wi' the blink o' his e'e.

He was nae a cooper, a common tub-hooper,
    The most o' his trade lay in pleasin' the fair;
He hoopt them, he coopt them, he bort them, he plugt
        them.
    An' a' sent for Sandie when out o' repair.

For a twelvemonth or sae this youth was respected,
    An' he was as bisie, as weel he could be;
But bis'ness increas'd so, that some were neglected,
    Which ruin'd trade in the town o' Dundee.

A baillie's fair daughter had wanted a coopin',
    An' Sandie was sent for, as oft time was he,
He yerkt her sae hard that she sprung an end-hoopin',
    Which banish'd poor Sandie frae bonny Dundee.

WILL YE NA, CAN YE NA, LET ME BE

TUNE: *I ha'e laid a herrin' in sa't*

ᴐ◈ᴐ

There liv'd a wife in Whistle-cockpen,
   Will ye na, can ye na, let me be,
She brews gude yill for gentleman,
   And ay she waggit it wantonlie.

The night blew sair wi' wind and weet,
   Will ye na, can ye na, let me be,
She shaw'd the traveller ben to sleep,
   And ay she waggit it wantonlie.

She saw a sight below his sark,
   Will ye na, can ye na, let me be,
She wadna wanted it for a mark,
   And ay she waggit it wantonlie.

She saw a sight aboon his knee,
   Will ye na, can ye na, let me be,
She wadna wanted it for three,
   And ay she waggit it wantonlie.

O whare live ye, and what's your trade?
   Will ye na, can ye na, let me be,
I am a thresher gude, he said,
   And ay she waggit it wantonlie.

And that's my flail and workin' graith,
   Will ye na, can ye na, let me be,
And noble tools, quo' she, by my faith!
   And ay she waggit it wantonlie.

I wad gie a browst, the best I hae,
  Will ye na, can ye na, let me be,
For a gude darge o' graith like thae,
  And ay she waggit it wantonlie.

I wad sell the hair frae aff my tail,
  Will ye na, can ye na, let me be,
To buy our Andrew siccan a flail,
  And ay she waggit it wantonlie.

ELLIBANKS

TUNE: *Gillicrankie*

⌀❖⌀

Ellibanks and Ellibraes,
　My blessin's ay befa' them,
Tho' I wish I had brunt a' my claes,
　The first time e'er I saw them:
Your succar kisses were sae sweet,
　Deil d—n me gin I ken, man,
How ye gart me lay my legs aside,
　And lift my sark mysel, man.

There's no a lass in a' the land,
　Can f—k sae weel as I can;
Louse down your breeks, lug out your wand,
　Hae ye nae mind to try, man:
For ye're the lad that wears the breeks,
　And I'm the lass that loes ye;
Deil rive my c—t to candle-wicks,
　Gif ever I refuse ye!!!

I'll clasp my arms about your neck,
　As souple as an eel, jo;
I'll cleek my houghs about your a—e,
　As I were gaun to speel, jo;
I'll cleek my houghs about your a—e,
　As I were gaun to speel, jo;
And if Jock thief he should slip out,
　I'll ding him wi' my heel, jo.

Green be the broom on Ellibraes,
    And yellow be the gowan!
My wame it fistles ay like flaes,
    As I come o'er the knowe, man:
There I lay glowran to the moon,
    Your mettle wadna daunton,
For hard your hurdies hotch'd aboon,
    While I below lay panting.

COMIN' THRO' THE RYE

O gin a body meet a body,
  Comin' throu the rye;
Gin a body f—k a body,
  Need a body cry.

    Comin' thro' the rye, my jo,
      An' comin' thro' the rye;
    She fand a staun o' staunin' graith,
      Comin' thro' the rye.

Gin a body meet a body,
  Comin' thro' the glen;
Gin a body f—k a body,
  Need the warld ken.

Gin a body meet a body,
  Comin' thro' the grain;
Gin a body f—k a body,
  C—t's a body's ain.

Gin a body meet a body,
  By a body's sel,
What na body f—s a body,
  Wad a body tell.

Mony a body meets a body,
  They dare na weel avow;
Mony a body f—s a body,
  Ye wadna think it true.

AS I CAM O'ER THE CAIRNEY MOUNT

TUNE: *Highland Laddie*

As I cam o'er the Cairney mount,
   And down amang the blooming heather,
The Highland laddie drew his durk
   And sheath'd it in my wanton leather.

     O my bonnie, bonnie Highland lad,
     My handsome, charming Highland laddie;
     When I am sick and like to die,
     He'll row me in his Highland plaiddie.

With me he play'd his warlike pranks,
   And on me boldly did adventure,
He did attack me on both flanks,
   And pushed me fiercely in the centre.

A furious battle then began,
   Wi' equal courage and desire,
Altho' he struck me three to one,
   I stood my ground and receiv'd his fire.

But our ammunition being spent,
   And we quite out o' breath an' sweating,
We did agree with ae consent,
   To fight it out at the next meeting.

JOHN ANDERSON, MY JO

John Anderson, my jo, John,
   I wonder what ye mean,
To lie sae lang i' the mornin',
   And sit sae late at e'en?
Ye'll bleer a' your een, John,
   And why do ye so?
Come sooner to your bed at een,
   John Anderson, my jo.

John Anderson, my jo, John,
   When first that ye began,
Ye had as good a tail-tree,
   As ony ither man;
But now its waxen wan, John,
   And wrinkles to and fro;
[I've t] wa gae-ups for ae gae-down,
   [John] Anderson, my jo.

[I'm ba]ckit like a salmon,
   [I'm] breastit like a swan;
My wame it is a down-cod,
   My middle ye may span:
Frae my tap-knot to my tae, John,
   I'm like the new-fa'n snow;
And it's a' for your convenience,
   John Anderson, my jo.

O it is a fine thing
    To keep out o'er the dyke;
But its a meikle finer thing,
    To see your hurdies fyke;
To see your hurdies fyke, John,
    And hit the rising blow;
It's then I like your chanter-pipe,
    John Anderson, my jo.

When ye come on before, John,
    See that ye do your best;
When ye begin to haud me,
    See that ye grip me fast;
See that ye grip me fast, John,
    Until that I cry "Oh!"
Your back shall crack or I do that,
    John Anderson, my jo.

John Anderson, my jo, John,
    Ye're welcome when ye please;
It's either in the warm bed
    Or else aboon the claes:
Or ye shall hae the horns, John,
    Upon your head to grow;
An' that's the cuckold's mallison,
    John Anderson, my jo.

DUNCAN DAVIDSON

✧

There was a lass, they ca'd her Meg,
   An' she gaed o'er the muir to spin;
She fee'd a lad to lift her leg,
   They ca'd him Duncan Davidson.
                  Fal, lal, &c.

Meg had a muff and it was rough,
   Twas black without and red within,
An' Duncan, case he got the cauld,
   He stole his highland p——e in.
                  Fal, lal, &c.

Meg had a muff, and it was rough,
   And Duncan strak tway handfu' in;
She clasp'd her heels about his waist,
   "I thank you Duncan! Yerk it in!!!"
                  Fal, lal, &c.

Duncan made her hurdies dreep,
   In Highland wrath, then Meg did say;
O gang he east, or gang he west,
   His ba's will no be dry today.

THE PLOUGHMAN

The ploughman he's a bonnie lad,
　His mind is ever true, jo;
His garters knit below the knee,
　His bonnet it is blue, jo.

　　Sing up wi't a', the ploughman lad,
　　And hey the merry ploughman;
　　O' a' the trades that I do ken,
　　Commend me to the ploughman.

As wakin' forth upon a day,
　I met a jolly ploughman,
I tald him I had lands to plough,
　If he wad prove true, man.

He says, my dear, tak ye nae fear,
　I'll fit you till a hair jo;
I'll cleave it up, and hit it down,
　And water-furrow't fair, jo.

I hae three ousen in my plough,
　Three better ne'er plough'd ground, jo.
The foremost ox is lang and sma',
　The twa are plump and round, jo.

Then he wi' speed did yoke his plough,
　Which by a gaud was driven, jo!
But when he wan between the stilts,
　I thought I was in heaven, jo!

But the foremost ox fell in the fur,
    The tither twa did founder;
The ploughman lad he breathless grew,
    In faith it was nae wonder.

But a sykie risk, below the hill,
    The plough she took a stane, jo,
Which gart the fire flee frae the sock,
    The ploughman gied a grane, jo.

I hae plough'd east, I hae plough'd west,
    In weather foul and fair, jo;
But the sairest ploughing e'er I plough'd,
    Was ploughing amang hair, jo.

    Sing up wi't a', and in wi't a',
    And hey my merry ploughman;
    O' a' the trades, and crafts I ken,
    Commend me to the ploughman.

ANDREW AN' HIS CUTTIE GUN

When a' the lave gaed to their bed,
  And I sat up to clean the shoon,
O wha think ye cam jumpin' ben,
  But Andrew and his cuttie gun.

  Blythe, blythe, blythe was she,
  Blythe was she but and ben,
  An' weel she lo'ed it in her neive,
  But better when it slippit in.

Or e'er I wist he laid me back,
  And up my gamon to my chin,
And ne'er a word to me he spak,
  But liltit out his cutty gun.

The bawsent bitch she left the whalps,
  And hunted round us at the fun,
As Andrew fodgel'd wi his a——e,
  And fir'd at me the cuttie gun.

O some delights in cuttie stoup,
  And some delights in cuttie-mun,
But my delight's an a——elins coup,
  Wi' Andrew an' his cuttie gun.

O CAN YE LABOUR LEE, YOUNG MAN?

TUNE: *Sir Arch. Grant's Strathspey*

❍❖❍

I fee'd a man at Martinmas,
    Wi arle pennies three;
But a' the fau't I had to him,
    He coudna labour lee.

      O can ye labour lee, young man,
        O can ye labour lee;
      Gae back the road ye cam agin,
        Ye shall never scorn me.

A stibble rig is easy plough'd,
    An' fallow land is free;
But what a silly coof is he,
    That canna labour lee.

The spretty bush, an' benty knowe,
    The ploughman points his sock in,
He sheds the roughness, lays it by,
    An' bauldly ploughs his yokin'.

IV

❧

COLLECTED
BY BURNS

THE REELS O' BOGIE

TUNE: *Cauld Kail in Aberdeen*

You lads and lasses all that dwell
  In the town of Strathbogie,
Whene'er you meet a pretty lass,
  Be sure you tip her cogie.
The lads and lasses toy and kiss,
  The lads ne'er think it is amiss
To bang the holes whereout they piss,
  And that's the reels o' Bogie.

There's Kent, and Keen, and Aberdeen,
  And the town of Strathbogie,
Where every lad may have his lass,
  Now that I've got my cogie.
They spread wide their snow-white thighs
  And roll about their wanton eyes,
And when they see your pintle rise
  They'll dance the reels o' Bogie.

A trooper going o'er the lea,
  He swore that he would steer me,
And long before the break of day,
  He giggled, goggled near me.
He put a stiff thing in my hand,
  I could not bear the banging o't
But long before he went away
  I suppled both the ends o't.

His pintle was of largest size,
  Indeed it was a banger,
He sought a prize between my thighs
  Till it became a hanger.

Had you but seen the wee bit skin
  He had to put his pintle in,
You'd sworn it was a chitterling
  Dancing the reels o' Bogie.

He turned about to fire again
  And give me t'other sally,
And as he fired I ne'er retired
  But received him in my alley.
His pebbles they went thump, thump,
  Against my little wanton rump,
But soon I left him but the stump
  To dance the reels o' Bogie.

Said I, young man, more you can't do,
  I think I've granted your desire,
By bobbing on my wanton clue,
  You see your pintle's all on fire.
When on my back I work like steel
  And bar the door with my left heel,
The more you f— the less I feel,
  And that's the reels o' Bogie.

JOCKEY WAS A BONNY LAD

TUNE: *John Roy Stewart's Strathspey*

My jockey is a bonny lad,
A dainty lad, a merry lad,
A neat sweet pretty little lad,
 An' just the lad for me.
For when we o'er the meadows stray,
He's ay sae lively ay sae gay,
An' aft right canty does he say,
 There's nane he loes like me.

An' he's ay huggin' ay dawtin',
Ay clappin', ay pressin',
Ay squeezin', ay kissin',
 An' winna let me be.

I met my lad the ither day,
Friskin' thro' a field o' hay,
Says he, dear Jenny, will ye stay,
 An' crack a while wi' me.
Na, Jockey lad, I darena stay,
My mither she'd miss me away;
Syne she'll flyte an' scauld a' day,
 An' play the diel wi' me.

But Jockey still continued, &c.

Hoot! Jockey, see my hair is down,
An' look you've torn a' my gown,
An' how will I gae thro' the town,
 Dear laddie tell to me.
He never minded what I said,

But wi' my neck an' bosom play'd;
Tho' I intreated, begg'd an' pray'd
  Him no to touzle me.

    But Jockey still continued
    Huggin', dawtin', clappin', squeezin',
    An' ay kissin', kissin', kissin',
      Till down cam we.

As breathless an' fatigued I lay,
In his arms among the hay,
My blood fast thro' my veins did play
  As he lay huggin' me;
I thought my breath wou'd never last,
For Jockey danc'd sae devilish fast;
But what cam o'er, I trow, at last,
  There diel ane kens but me.

    But soon he weari'd o' his dance,
    O' a' his jumpin' an' his prance,
    An' confess'd without romance,
      He was fain to let me be.

BLYTH WILL AN' BESSIE'S WEDDING

TUNE: *Roy's Wife*

◇❖◇

There was a weddin' o'er in Fife,
 An' mony ane frae Lothian at it;
Jean Vernor there maist lost hir life,
 For love o' Jamie Howden at it.

  Blyth Will an' Bessie's weddin',
  Blyth Will an' Bessie's weddin',
  Had I been Will, Bess had been mine,
  An' Bess an' I had made the weddin'.

Right sair she grat, an' wet her cheeks,
 An' naithing pleas'd that we cou'd gie her;
She tint her heart in Jeamie's breeks,
 It cam nae back to Lothian wi' her.

[Tam]mie Tamson too was there,
 Maggie Birnie was his dearie,
He pat it in amang the hair,
 An' puddled there till he was weary.

When e'enin' cam the town was thrang,
 An' beds were no to get for siller;
When e'er they fand a want o' room,
 They lay in pairs like bread an' butter.

Twa an' twa they made the bed,
 An' twa an' twa they lay the gither;
When they had na room enough,
 Ilk ane lap on aboon the tither.

THE LASS O' LIVISTON

The bonny lass o' Liviston,
   Her name ye ken, her name ye ken;
And ay the welcomer ye'll be,
   The farther ben, the farther ben,
And she has it written in her contract
   To lie her lane, to lie her lane,
And I hae written in my contract
   To claw her wame, to claw her wame.

The bonny lass o' Liviston,
   She's berry brown, she's berry brown;
An' ye winna true her lovely locks,
   Gae farther down, gae farther down.
She has a black and a rolling eye,
   And a dimplit chin, and a dimplit chin;
And no to prie her rosy lips,
   Wad be a sin, wad be a sin.

The bonny lass o' Liviston,
   Cam in to me, cam in to me;
I wat wi' baith ends o' the busk,
   I made me free, I made me free.
I laid her feet to my bed-stock,
   Her head to the wa', her head to the wa';
And I gied her her wee coat in her teeth,
   Her sark an' a', her sark an' a'.

HE'S HOY'D ME OUT O' LAUDERDALE

There liv'd a lady in Lauderdale,
  She lo'ed a fiddler fine;
She lo'ed him in her chamber,
  She held him in her mind;
She made his bed at her bed-stock,
  She said he was her brither;
But she's hoy'd him out o' Lauderdale,
  His fiddle and a' thegither.

First when I cam to Lauderdale,
  I had a fiddle gude,
My sounding-pin stood like the aik
  That grows in Lauder-wood;
But now my sounding-pin's gaen down,
  And tint the foot forever;
She's hoy'd me out o' Lauderdale,
  My fiddle and a' thegither.

First when I came to Lauderdale,
  Your Ladyship can declare,
I play'd a bow, a noble bow,
  As e'er was strung wi' hair;
But dow'na do's come o'er me now,
  And your Ladyship winna consider;
She's hoy'd me out o' Lauderdale,
  My fiddle and a' thegither.

ERROCK BRAE

TUNE: *Sir Alex. Don's Strathspey*

ᴏ❖ᴏ

O Errock stane, may never maid,
   A maiden by thee gae,
Nor e'er a stane o' stanin' graith,
   Gae stanin' o'er the brae.

     And tillin' Errock brae, young man,
       An' tillin' Errock brae,
      An open fur an' stanin' graith,
       Maun till the Errock brae.

As I sat by the Errock stane,
   Surveying far and near,
Up cam a Cameronian,
   Wi' a' his preaching gear.

He flang the Bible o'er the brae,
   Amang the rashy gerse;
But the solemn league and covenant
   He laid below my a——e.

But on the edge of Errock brae,·
   He gae me sic a sten,
That o'er, and o'er, and o'er we row'd,
   Till we cam to the glen.

Yet still his p——e held the grip,
   And still his b——s hang;
That a Synod cou'd na tell the a——e
   To whom they did belang.

A Prelate he loups on before,
   A Catholic behin',
But gie me a Cameronian,
   He'll m——w a body blin'.

YE HAE LIEN WRANG, LASSIE

TUNE: *Up and waur them a', Willie*

◦❖◦

Your rosy cheeks are turn'd sae wan,
   Ye're greener than the grass, lassie,
Your coatie's shorter by a span,
   Yet deil an inch the less, lassie.

     Ye hae lien wrang, lassie,
       Ye've lien a' wrang,
     Ye've lien in some unco bed,
       And wi' some unco man.

Ye've loot the pounie o'er the dyke,
   And he's been in the corn, lassie;
For ay the brose ye sup at e'en,
   Ye bock them or the morn, lassie.

Fu' lightly lap ye o'er the knowe,
   And thro' the wood ye sang, lassie;
But herryin' o' the foggie byke,
   I fear ye've got a stang, lassie.

COMIN' O'ER THE HILLS O' COUPAR

TUNE: *Ruffian's Rant*

ᴏ◇ᴏ

Donald Brodie met a lass,
  Comin' o'er the hills o' Coupar,
Donald wi' his Highland hand
  Graipit a' the bits about her.

    Comin' o'er the hills o' Coupar,
    Comin' o'er the hills o' Coupar,
    Donald in a sudden wrath
    He ran his Highland durk into her.

Weel I wat she was a quine,
  Wad made a body's mouth to water;
Our Mess John, wi's auld grey pow,
  His haly lips wad licket at her.

Up she started in a fright,
  Thro' the braes what she could bicker:
Let her gang, quo' Donald, now
  For in him's nerse * my shot is sicker.

Kate Mackie cam frae Parlon craigs,
  The road was foul twixt that an' Couper;
She shaw'd a pair o' handsome legs,
  When Highland Donald he o'ertook her.

    Comin' o'er the moor o' Couper,
    Comin' o'er the moor o' Couper,
    Donald fell in love wi' her
    An' row'd his Highland plaid about her.

They took them to the Logan steps
    An' set them down to rest thegither,
Donald laid her on her back
    An' fir'd a Highland pistol at her.

Lochleven Castle heard the rair,
    An' Falkland-house the echo sounded;
Highland Donald gae a stare,
    The lassie sigh'd, but was nae wounded.

*   *   *

* *him's nerse* =her arse; a joke at expense of Highlanders' traditional muddling of genders.

iii, 2.   what . . . bicker, i.e. as fast as she could.

HOW CAN I KEEP MY MAIDENHEAD?

TUNE: *The Birks o' Abergeldie*

How can I keep my maidenhead,
  My maidenhead, my maidenhead;
How can I keep my maidenhead,
  Among sae mony men, O.

The Captain bad a guinea for't,
  A guinea for't, a guinea for't;
The Captain bad a guinea for't,
  The Colonel he bad ten, O.

But I'll do as my minnie did,
  My minnie did, my minnie did;
But I'll do as my minnie did,
  For siller I'll hae nane, O.

I'll gie it to a bonie lad,
  A bonie lad, a bonie lad;
I'll gie it to a bonie lad,
  For just as gude again, O.

An auld moulie maidenhead,
  A maidenhead, a maidenhead;
An auld moulie maidenhead,
  The weary wark I ken, O.

The stretchin' o't, the strivin' o't,
  The borin' o't, the rivin' o't,
And ay the double drivin' o't,
  The farther ye gang ben, O.

WAD YE DO THAT?

TUNE: *John Anderson, my jo*

ᴏ❖ᴏ

Gudewife, when your gudeman's frae hame,
    Might I but be sae bauld,
As come to your bed-chamber,
    When winter nights are cauld;
As come to your bed-chamber,
    When nights are cauld and wat,
And lie in your gudeman's stead,
    Wad ye do that?

Young man, an ye should be so kind,
    When our gudeman's frae hame,
As come to my bed-chamber,
    Where I am laid my lane;
And lie in our gudeman's stead,
    I will tell you what,
He f—s me five times ilka night,
    Wad ye do that?

THERE CAM A CADGER

TUNE: *Clout the Cauldron*

◦◈◦

There cam a cadger out o' Fife,
    I watna how they ca'd him;
He play'd a trick to our gudewife,
    When fient a body bad him.

      Fal, lal, &c.

He took a lang thing stout and strang,
    An' strack it in her gyvel;
An' ay she swore she fand the thing
    Gae borin' by her nyvel.

      Fal, lal, &c.

JENNY MACRAW

TUNE: *The bonny moor-hen*

◯◈◯

Jenny Macraw was a bird o' the game,
An' mony a shot had been lows'd at her wame;
Be't a lang bearing arrow, or the sharp-rattlin' hail,
Still, whirr! she flew off wi' the shot in her tail.

Jenny Macraw to the mountains she's gaen,
Their leagues and their covenants a' she has taen;
My head now, and heart now, quo' she, are at rest,
An' for my poor c—t, let the deil do his best.

Jenny Macraw on a midsummer morn,
She cut off her c—t and she hang't on a thorn;
There she loot it hing for a year and a day,
But, oh! how look'd her a—e when her c—twas away.

OUR GUDEWIFE'S SAE MODEST

TUNE: *John Anderson, my jo*

Our gudewife's sae modest,
  When she is set at meat,
A laverock's leg, or a tittling's wing,
  Is mair than she can eat;
But, when she's in her bed at e'en,
  Between me and the wa';
She is a glutton deevil,
  She swallows c—s an a'.

SUPPER IS NA READY

TUNE: *Clout the Cauldron*

Roseberry to his lady says,
  "My hinnie and my succour,
"O shall we do the thing you ken,
  "Or shall we take our supper?"
    Fal, lal, &c.

Wi' modest face, sae fu' o' grace,
  Replied the bonny lady;
"My noble lord do as you please,
  "But supper is na ready."
    Fal, lal, &c.

YON, YON, YON, LASSIE

TUNE: *Ruffian's Rant*

✧

I never saw a silken gown,
But I wad kiss the sleeve o't;
I never saw a maidenhead
That I wad spier the leave o't.

O, yon, yon, yon, lassie,
Yon, yon, yon;
I never met a bonie lass
But what wad play at yon.

Tell nae me, o' Meg my wife,
That crowdie has na savour;
But gie to me a bonie lass
An' let me steal the favour.

Gie me her I kis't yestreen,
I vow but she was handsome,
For ilka birss upon her c—t,
Was worth a royal ransom.

An' yon, yon, yon, lassie,
Yon, yon, yon,
I never saw a bonie lass
But what wad do yon.

THE YELLOW, YELLOW YORLIN'

TUNE: *Bonnie beds of roses*

ᵒ◆ᵒ

It fell on a day, in the flow'ry month o' May,
  All on a merry merry mornin',
I met a pretty maid, an' unto her I said,
  I wad fain fin' your yellow yellow yorlin'.

O no, young man, says she, you're a stranger to me,
  An' I am anither man's darlin',
Wha has baith sheep an' cows, that's feedin' in the
      hows,
  An' a cock for my yellow yellow yorlin'.

But, if I lay you down upon the dewy ground,
  You wad nae be the waur ae farthing;
An' that happy, happy man, he never wou'd ken
  That I play'd wi' your yellow yellow yorlin'.

O fie, young man, says she, I pray you let me be,
  I wad na for five pound sterling;
My mither wad gae mad, an' sae wad my dad,
  If you play'd wi' my yellow yellow yorlin'.

But I took her by the waist, an' laid her down in haste,
  For a' her squakin' and squalin';
The lassie soon grew tame, an' bade me come again
  For to play wi' her yellow yellow yorlin'.

SHE GRIPET AT THE GIRTEST O'T

TUNE: *East Nook of Fife*

❧❖❧

Our bride flate, and our bride flang,
But lang before the laverock sang,
She pay't him twice for every bang,
   And gripet at the girtest o't.

Our bride turn'd her to the wa',
But lang before the cock did craw,
She took him by the b——ks and a',
   And gripet at the girtest o't.

YE'SE GET A HOLE TO HIDE IT IN

TUNE: *Waukin' o' the Fauld*

ᴏ❖ᴏ

O will ye speak at our town,
   As ye come frae the fair?
And ye'se get a hole to hide it in,
   Ye'se get a hole to hide it in;
Will ye speak at our town
   As ye come frae the fair,
Ye'se get a hole to hide it in,
   Will haud it a' and mair.

O haud awa your hand, Sir,
   Ye gar me ay think shame;
An' ye'se get a hole to hide it in;
   Ye'se get a hole to hide it in;
O haud awa your hand, Sir,
   Ye gar me ay think shame;
An' ye'se get a hole to hide it in,
   An' think yoursel at hame.

O will ye let abee, Sir;
   Toots! now, ye've rivt my sark,
An' ye'se get a hole to hide it in,
   Ye'se get a hole to hide it in;
O will ye let abee, Sir;
   Toots! now, ye've reft my sark;
An' ye'se get a hole to hide it in,
   Whare ye may work your wark.

O haud awa your hand, Sir,
   Ye're like to pit me daft;
And ye'se get a hole to hide it in,
   Ye'se get a hole to hide it in;
O had awa your hand, Sir,
   Ye're like to put me daft;
An' ye'se get a hole to hide it in,
   To keep it warm and saft.

O had it in your hand, Sir,
   Till I get up my claes,
An' ye'se get a hole to hide it in,
   Ye'se get a hole to hide it in;
O had it in your hand, Sir,
   Till I get up my claes;
An' ye'se get a hole to hide it in,
   To keep it frae the flaes.

DUNCAN MACLEERIE

TUNE: *Jocky Macgill*

Duncan Macleerie and Janet his wife,
They gaed to Kilmarnock to buy a new knife;
But instead of a knife they coft but a bleerie;
We're very weel saird. quo' Duncan Macleerie.

Duncan Macleerie has got a new fiddle,
It's a' strung wi' hair, and a hole in the middle;
An' ay when he plays on't, his wife looks sae cheary,
Very weel done, Duncan, quo' Janet Macleerie.

Duncan he play'd 'till his bow it grew greasy;
Janet grew fretfu', and unco uneasy.
Hoot, quo' she, Duncan, ye're unco soon weary;
Play us a pibroch, quo' Janet Macleerie.

Duncan Macleerie play'd on the harp,
An' Janet Macleerie danc'd in her sark;
Her sark it was short, her c—t it was hairy,
Very weel danc'd, Janet, quo' Duncan Macleerie.

THEY TOOK ME TO THE HALY BAND

TUNE: *Clout the Cauldron*

ᗡ❖ᗡ

They took me to the haly band,
   For playing bye my wife, Sir;
And lang and sair they lectur'd me,
   For hadin' sic a life, Sir.

I answer'd in na mony words,
   "What deel needs a' this clatter;
"As lang as she cou'd keep the grip
   "I aye was m——g at her."

THE MODIEWARK

TUNE: *O for ane an' twenty, Tam*

❤❤❤

The modiewark has done me ill,
And below my apron has biggit a hill;
I maun consult some learned clark
About this wanton modiewark.

    An' O the wanton modiewark,
    The weary wanton modiewark;
    I maun consult some learned clark
    About this wanton modiewark.

O first it gat between my taes,
Out o'er my garter niest it gaes;
At length it crap below my sark,
The weary wanton modiewark.

This modiewark, tho' it be blin';
If ance its nose you lat it in,
Then to the hilts, within a crack
It's out o' sight, the modiewark.

When Marjorie was made a bride,
An' Willy lay down by her side,
Syne nocht was hard, when a' was dark,
But kicking at the modiewark.

KEN YE NA OUR LASS, BESS?

TUNE: *Auld Sir Symon*

⤫

O ken ye na our lass, Bess?
An' ken ye na our lass, Bess?
Between her lily white thies
She's biggit a magpie's nest.

An' ken ye na our lad, Tam?
An' ken ye na our lad, Tam?
He's on o' a three-fitted stool,
An' up to the nest he clamb.

An' what did he there, think ye?
An' what did he there, think ye?
He brak a' the eggs o' the nest,
An' the white's ran down her thie.

WHA THE DEIL CAN HINDER THE WIND TO BLAW?

TUNE: *Wat ye wha I met yestreen?*

❦

It fell about the blythe new-year,
  When days are short and nights are lang,
Ae bonie night, the starns were clear,
  An' frost beneath my fit-stead rang;
I heard a carlin cry, "relief!"
  Atweesh her trams a birkie lay;
But he wan a quarter in her beef,
  For a' the jirts the carlin gae.

She heav'd to; and he strak frae,
  As he wad nail'd the carlin thro';
An' ilka f—t the carlin gae,
  It wad hae fill'd a pockie fou;
Temper your tail, the young man cried,
  Temper your tail by Venus' law!
Double your dunts, the dame replied,
  Wha the deil can hinder the wind to blaw?

WE'RE A' GAUN SOUTHIE, O

TUNE: *The Merry Lads of Ayr*

⟳◆⟳

Callum cam to Campbell's court,
  An' saw ye e'er the make o't;
Pay'd twenty shillings for a thing,
  An' never got a straik o't.

  We're a' gaun southie, O.
  We're a' gaun there;
  An' we're a' gaun to Mauchlin fair,
  To sell our pickle hair.

Pay'd twenty shillings for a quine,
  Her name was Kirsty Lauchlan;
But Callum took her by the c—t,
  Before the laird o' Mauchline.

Callum cam to Kirsty's door,
  Says, Kirsty are ye sleepin'?
No sae soun as ye wad trow,
  Ye'se get the thing ye're seekin'.

Callum had a peck o' meal,
  Says, Kirsty, will ye draik it?
She whippet off her wee white-coat,
  An' birket at it nakit.

Bonie lassie, braw lassie,
  Will ye hae a soger?
Then she took up her duddie sark,
  An' he shot in his Roger.

Kind kimmer Kirsty,
   I loe wi' a' my heart, O,
An' when there's ony p——s gaun,
   She'll ay get a part, O.

CUDDIE THE COOPER

TUNE: *Bonny Dundee*

～◇～

There was a cooper they ca'd him Cuddy,
   He was the best cooper that ever I saw;
He came to girth our landlady's tubbie,
   He bang'd her buttocks again the wa'.

Cooper quo' she, hae ye ony mony?
   The deevil a penny, quo' Cuddy, at a'!
She took out her purse, an' she gied him a guinea,
   For banging her buttocks again the wa'.

NAE HAIR ON'T

TUNE: *Gillicrankie*

◇

Yestreen I wed a lady fair,
  And ye wad believe me,
On her c—t there grows nae hair,
  That's the thing that grieves me.

It vexed me sair, it plagu'd me sair,
  It put me in a passion,
To think that I had wad a wife,
  Whase c—t was out o' fashion.

THERE'S HAIR ON'T

TUNE: *Push about the jorum*

O, ere yestreen I stented graith,
    An' labor'd lang an' sair on't;
But fient a work, na work wad it,
    There's sic a crap o' hair on't.

        There's hair on't, there's hair on't,
        There's thretty thrave an' mair on't;
        But gin I live to anither year,
        I'll tether my grey naigs on't.

An' up the glen there rase a knowe,
    Below the knowe a lair on't,
I maist had perish'd, fit an' horse,
    I could na see for hair on't.

But I'll plant a stake into the flowe,
    That ploughmen may tak care on't;
An' lay twa steppin'-stanes below,
    An' syne I'll cowe the hair on't.

THE LASSIE GATH'RING NITS

TUNE: *O the broom*

ᴼ❖ᴼ

There was a lass, and a bonie lass,
　A gath'ring nits did gang;
She pu'd them heigh, she pu'd them laigh,
　She pu'd them whare they hang.

Till tir'd at length, she laid her down,
　An' sleept the wood amang;
Whan by there cam three lusty lads,
　Three lusty lads an' strang.

The first did kiss her rosy lips,
　He thought it was nae wrang;
The second lous'd her bodice fair,
　Fac'd up wi' London whang.

An' what the third did to the lass,
　I's no put in this sang;
But the lassie wauken'd in a fright,
　An' says, I hae sleept lang.

THE LINKIN' LADDIE

TUNE: *Push about the jorum*

ᗞ❖ᗞ

Waes me that e'er I made your bed!
   Waes me that e'er I saw ye!
For now I've lost my maidenhead,
   An' I ken na how they ca' ye.

My name's weel kend in my ain countrie,
   They ca' me the linkin' laddie;
An' ye had na been as willing as I,
   Shame fa' them wad e'er hae bade ye.

JOHNIE SCOTT

TUNE: *O the broom*

Whare will we get a coat to Johnie Scott,
    Amang us maidens a'?
Whare will we get a coat to Johnie Scott,
    To mak the laddie braw:

There's your c—t-hair, and there's my c—t hair,
    An' we'll twine it wondrous sma';
An' if waft be scarce, we'll cowe our a—e,
    To mak him kilt an' a'.

MADGIE CAM TO MY BED-STOCK

TUNE: *Clout the Cauldron*

༶❖༶

Madgie cam to my bed-stock,
   To see gif I was waukin;
I pat my han' atweesh her feet,
   An' fand her wee bit maukin.
      Fal, lal, &c.

C—t it was the sowen-pat,
   An' p——e was the ladle;
B—ks were the serving-men
   That waited at the table.
      Fal, lal, &c.

O GIN I HAD HER

TUNE: *Saw ye na my Peggy*

O gin I had her,
Ay gin I had her,
O gin I had her,
    Black altho' she be.
I wad lay her bale,
I'd gar her spew her kail;
She ne'er soud keep a mail,
    Till she dandl'd it on her knee.

She says, I am light
To manage matters right,
That I've nae might or weight
    To fill a lassie's ee;
But wad she tak a yokin',
I wad put a c—k in;
A quarter o't to flocken,
    I wad frankly gie.

HE TILL'T AND SHE TILL'T

TUNE: *Maggie Lauder*

He till't, and she till't,
    An' a' to mak a lad again;
The auld beld carl,
    Whan he wan on did nod again;
An' he dang, an' she flang,
    An' a' to mak a laddie o't;
But he bor'd and she roar'd,
    An' coudna mak a lassie o't.

V

⌀◆⌀

ALIEN

MODES

[Poems in which Burns abandoned his usual folksong style and dressed his subject in conventional poetic verse forms.]

TWEEDMOUTH TOWN

◦◈◦

Near Tweedmouth town there liv'd three maids,
    Who used to tope good ale;
An' there likewise liv'd three wives,
    Who sometimes wagged their tale;
They often met, to tope an' chat,
    And tell odd tales of men;
[Cr]ying, when shall we meet again, an' again,
    [Cr]ying, when shall we meet again.

Not far from these there liv'd three widows,
    With complexions wan an' pale,
Who seldom used to tope an' bouse,
    An' seldom wagged their tale.
They sigh'd, they pin'd, they griev'd, they whin'd,
    An' often did complain,
Shall we, quo they, ne'er sport or play
    Nor wag our tails again, an' again.

Nine northern lads with their Scots plaids,
    By the Union, British call'd,
All nine-inch men, to a bousing came,
    Wi' their brawny backs I'm tald.
They all agreed, to cross the Tweed,
    An' ease them of their pain;
They laid them all down,
    An' they f—k'd them all round,
An' cross'd the Tweed again, an' again.

THE BOWER OF BLISS

TUNE: *Logan Water*

ᴏ᭺ᴏ

Whilst others to thy bosom rise,
And paint the glories of thine eyes,
Or bid thy lips and cheeks disclose,
The unfading bloom of Eden's rose.
Less obvious charms my song inspire,
Which fell, not fear we most admire—
Less obvious charms, not less divine,
I sing that lovely bower of thine.

Rich gem! worth India's wealth alone,
How much pursued how little known;
Tho' rough its face, tho' dim its hue,
It soils the lustre of Peru.
The vet'ran such a prize to gain,
Might all the toils of war sustain;
The devotee forsake his shrine,
To venerate that bower of thine.

When the stung heart feels keen desire,
And through each vein pours liquid fire:
When with flush'd cheeks and burning eyes,
Thy lover to thy bosom flies;
Believe, dear maid, believe my vow,
By Venus' self, I swear, 'tis true!
More bright the higher beauties shine,
Illum'd by that strange bower of thine.

What thought sublime, what lofty strain
Its wond'rous virtues can explain?
No place how'er remote, can be
From its intense attraction free:
Tho' more elastic far than steel,
Its force ten thousand needles feel;
Pleas'd their high temper to resign,
In that magnetic bower of thine.

Irriguous vale, embrown'd with shades,
Which no intrinsic storm pervades!
Soft clime, where native summer glows,
And nectar's living current flows!
Not Tempe's vale, renowned of yore,
Of charms could boast such endless store;
More than Elysian sweets combine,
To grace that smiling bower of thine.

O, may no rash invader stain,
Love's warm, sequestered virgin fane!
For me alone let gentle fate,
Preserve the dear august retreat!
Along its banks when shall I stray?
Its beauteous landscape when survey?
How long in fruitless anguish pine,
Nor view unvail'd that bower of thine?

O! let my tender, trembling hand,
The awful gate of life expand!
With all its wonders feast my sight;
Dear prelude to immense delight!
Till plung'd in liquid joy profound,
The dark unfathom'd deep I sound;
All panting on thy breast recline,
And, murmuring, bless that bower of thine.

THE PLENIPOTENTIARY

TUNE: *The Terrible Law* or *Shawnbuee*

ᐤ❖ᐤ

The Dey of Algiers, when afraid of his ears,
A messenger sent to our court, sir,
As he knew in our state the women had weight,
He chose one well hung for the sport, sir.
He searched the Divan till he found out a man
Whose b—— were heavy and hairy,
And he lately came o'er from the Barbary shore
As the great Plenipotentiary.

When to England he came, with his p—— in a flame,
He showed it his Hostess on landing,
Who spread its renown thro' all parts of the town,
As a pintle past all understanding.
So much there was said of its snout and its head,
That they called it the great Janissary;
Not a lady could sleep till she got a sly peep
At the great Plenipotentiary.

As he rode in his coach, how the whores did approach,
And stared, as if stretched on a tenter;
He drew every eye of the dames that passed by,
Like the sun to its wonderful centre.
As he passed thro' the town not a window was down,
And the maids hurried out to the area,
The children cried, "Look, there's the man with the
    cock,
That's the great Plenipotentiary."

When he came to the Court, oh, what giggle and sport,
Such squinting and squeezing to view him,
What envy and spleen in the women were seen,
All happy and pleased to get to him.
They vowed from their hearts, if men of such parts
Were found on the coast of Barbary,
'Tis a shame not to bring a whole guard for the King,
Like the great Plenipotentiary.

The dames of intrigue formed their c—— in a league,
To take him in turns like good folk, sir;
The young misses' plan to was catch as catch can,
And all were resolved on a stroke, sir.
The cards to invite flew by thousands each night,
With bribes to the old secretary,
And the famous Eclipse was not let for more leaps
Than the great Plenipotentiary.

When his name was announced, how the women all
    bounced,
And their blood hurried up to their faces;
He made them all itch from navel to breech,
And their bubbies burst out all their laces;
There was such damned work to be f—— by the Turk,
That nothing their passion could vary;
All the nations [?matrons] fell sick for the Barbary
    p——
Of the great Plenipotentiary.

A Duchess whose Duke made her ready to puke,
With fumbling and f—— all night, sir,
Being first for the prize, was so pleased with its size,
That she begged for to stroke its big snout, sir.
My stars! cried her Grace, its head's like a mace,
'Tis as high as the Corsican Fairy;

I'll make up, please the pigs, for dry bobs and frigs,
With the great Plenipotentiary.

And now to be bor'd by this Ottoman Lord
Came a Virgin far gone in the wane, sir,
She resolved for to try, tho' her c—— was so dry,
That she knew it must split like a cane, sir.
True it was as she spoke, it gave way at each stroke,
But oh, what a woeful quandary!
With one terrible thrust her old piss-bladder burst
On the great Plenipotentiary.

The next to be tried was an Alderman's Bride,
With a c—— that would swallow a turtle,
She had horned the dull brows of her worshipful
    spouse,
Till they sprouted like Venus's myrtle.
Thro' thick and thro' thin, bowel deep he dashed in,
Till her c—— frothed like cream in a dairy,
And expressed by loud farts she was strained in all
    parts
By the great Plenipotentiary.

The next to be kissed, on the Plenipo's list,
Was a delicate Maiden of Honor,
She screamed at the sight of his p——, in a fright,
Tho' she'd had the whole palace upon her.
O Lord, she said, what a p—— for a maid!
Do, pray, come look at it, Cary!
But I *will* have one drive, if I'm ripped up alive,
By the great Plenipotentiary.

Two sisters next came, Peg and Molly by name,
Two ladies of very high breeding,
Resolved one should try, while the other stood by
And watch the amusing proceeding.
Peg swore by the gods that the Mussulman's cods
Were as big as both buttocks of Mary;
Molly cried with a grunt, he has ruined my c—
With his great Plenipotentiary.

The next for this plan was an old Haridan,
Who had swallowed huge p—— from each nation,
With over much use she had broken the sluice
'Twixt her —— and its lower relation.
But he stuck her so full that she roared like a bull,
Crying out she was bursting and weary,
So tight was she stuck by this wonderful f——
Of the great Plenipotentiary.

The next for a shag came the new Yankee flag;
Tho' lanky and scraggy in figure,
She was fond of the quid, for she had been well rid
From Washington down to a nigger.
Oh my! such a size! I guess it's first prize,
It's a wonder, quite next Ni-a-gary;
W-a-l-l, now I'm in luck, stranger, let's f——,
Bully for the great Plenipotentiary.

All heads were bewitched and longed to be stitched,
Even babies would languish and linger,
And the boarding-school Miss, as she sat down to piss,
Drew a Turk on the floor with her finger.
For fancied delight, they all clubbed for a shite,
To frig in the school necessary,
And the Teachers from France f—— à la distance
With the great Plenipotentiary.

Each sluice-c——d bawd, who'd been s——d abroad
Till her premises gaped like a grave, sir,
Found luck was so thick, she could feel the **Turk's**
    p——,
Tho' all others were lost in her cave, sir.
The nymphs of the stage did his ramrod engage,
Made him free of their gay seminary;
And the Italian Signors opened all their back doors
To the great Plenipotentiary.

Then of love's sweet reward, measured out by the yard,
The Turk was most blest of mankind, sir,
For his powerful dart went right home to the heart,
Whether stuck in before or behind, sir.
But no pencil can draw this great-pintled Bashaw,
Then let each c—— loving contemporary,
As cocks of the game, let's drink to the name
Of the great Plenipotentiary.

UNA'S LOCK

⌒◈⌒

'Twas on a sweet morning,
    When violets were a-springing,
The dew the meads adorning,
    The larks melodious singing;
The rose-trees, by each breeze,
    Were gently wafted up and down,
And the primrose, that then blows,
    Bespangled nature's verdant gown.
The purling rill, the murmuring stream,
    Stole gently through the lofty grove:
Such was the time when Darby stole
    Out to meet his barefoot love.

Tol, lol, &c.

Sweet Una was the tightest,
    Genteelest of the village dames;
Her eyes were the brightest
    That e'er set youthful heart in flames.
Her lover to move her
    By every art in man essay'd
In ditty, for pity,
    This lovely maid he often prayed,
But she, perverse, his suit deni'd.
    Sly Darby, being enraged at this,
Resolv'd when next they met to seize
    The lock that scatters Una's piss.

Tol, lol, &c.

Beneath a lofty spreading oak
    She sat with can and milking pail;

From lily hands at each stroke
　　In flowing streams the milk did steal.
With peeping, and creeping,
　　Sly Darby now comes on apace;
In raptures the youth sees
　　The blooming beauties of her face.
Fir'd with her charms, he now resolv'd
　　No longer to delay his bliss,
But instantly to catch the lock
　　That scatters pretty Una's piss.

Tol, lol, &c.

Upon her back he laid her,
　　Turned up her smock so lily white;
With joy the youth surveyed her,
　　Then gaped with wonder and delight.
Her thighs they were so snowy fair,
　　And just between appeared a crack;
The lips red, and overspread
　　With curling hair of jetty black.
Transported now, Darby beholds
　　The sum of all his promised bliss,
And instantly he caught the lock
　　That scatters pretty Una's piss.

Tol, lol, &c.

Within his arms he seized her,
　　And pressed her to his panting breast;
What more could have appeased her,
　　But oaths which Darby meant in jest.
He swore he'd but adore her,
　　And to her ever constant prove;

He'd wed her, he'd bed her,
  And none on earth but her he'd love.
With vows like those he won her o'er,
  And hoped she'd take it not amiss
If he presumed to catch the lock
  That scatters pretty Una's piss.
        Tol, lol, &c.

His cock it stood erected,
  His breeches down about his heels,
And what he long expected
  He now with boundless rapture feels.
Now entered, and concentred,
  The beauteous maid lay in a trance,
His bullocks went like elbows
  Of fiddlers in a country dance.
The melting Una, now she cries,
  I'd part with life for joy like this;
With showers of bliss they jointly oiled
  The lock that scatters Una's piss.
        Tol, lol, &c.

VI

LIBEL

SUMMONS

[This poem, written by Burns for the Tarbolton Bachelors' Club in 1786, is also known as *The Court of Equity* and *The Fornicator's Court.*]

LIBEL SUMMONS

In Truth and Honor's name, AMEN.—
Know all men by these presents plain.—

This twalt o' May at M[auchli]ne given;
The year 'tween eighty five an' seven;
We, FORNICATORS by profession,
As per extractum from each Session;[1]

And by our BRETHREN constituted,
A COURT of Equity deputed:
With special authoris'd direction,
To take beneath our strict protection,
The stays-unlacing, quondam maiden,
With growing life and anguish laden;
Who by the Scoundrel is deny'd
Who led her thoughtless steps aside.—

The knave who takes a private stroke
Beneath his sanctimonious cloke:
(The Coof wha stan's on clishmaclavers
When lasses hafflins offer favors)

All who in any way or manner
Distain the FORNICATOR's honor,
We take cognisance there anent
The proper Judges competent.—
First, Poet B[urns], he takes the CHAIR,
Allow'd by all, his title's fair;
And past nem. con. without dissension,
He has a DUPLICATE pretension.—

The second, Sm[i]th, our worthy FISCAL,
To cowe each pertinacious rascal;
In this, as every other state,
His merit is conspicuous great;
R[ichmo]nd the third, our trusty CLERK,
Our minutes regular to mark,
And sit dispenser of the law,
In absence of the former twa.—
The fourth, our MESSENGER AT ARMS,
When failing all the milder terms,
Hunt[e]r, a hearty willing Brother,
Weel skill'd in dead an' living leather.—

Without preamble less or more said,
We, BODY POLITIC aforesaid,
With legal, due WHEREAS and WHEREFORE,
We are appointed here to care for
The int'rests of our Constituents,
And punish contravening Truants;
To keep a proper regulation
Within the lists of FORNICATION.—

WHEREAS, Our FISCAL, by petition,
Informs us there is strong suspicion
YOU, Coachman DOW, and Clockie BROWN,
Baith residenters in this town,
In other words, you, Jock and Sandie
Hae been at wark at HOUGHMAGANDIE;
And now when it is come to light,
The matter ye deny outright.—

You CLOCKIE BROWN, there's witness borne,
And affidavit made and sworne,
That ye hae rais'd a hurlie-burlie
In Maggy Mitchel's tirlie-whurlie.—

(And blooster'd at her regulator,
Till a' her wheels gang clitter-clatter.—)[1]

An' farther still, ye cruel Vandal,
A tale might e'en in Hell be scandal,
Ye've made repeated wicked tryals
With drugs an' draps in doctor's phials,
Mix'd, as ye thought, wi' fell infusion,
Your ain begotten wean to poosion.
An' yet ye are sae scant o' grace,
Ye daur set up your brazen face,
An' offer for to tak your aith,
Ye never lifted Maggie's claith.—
But tho' by Heaven an' Hell ye swear,
Laird Wilson's sclates can witness bear,
Ae e'ening of a M[auchli]ne fair,
That Maggie's masts, they saw them bare,
For ye had furl'd up her sails,
An' was at play at heads an' tails.—

You COACHMAN DOW are here indicted
To have, as publickly ye're wyted,
Been clandestinely upward-whirlan
The petticoats o' Maggie Borlan;
An' gied her canister a rattle,
That months to come it winna settle.—
An' yet ye offer your protest,
Ye never harry'd Maggie's nest;
Tho' it's weel-kend that, at her gyvle,
Ye hae gien mony a kytch an' kyvle.—

Then BROWN & DOW, above-design'd,
For clags and clauses there subjoin'd,
We COURT *aforesaid, cite & summon,*

That on the fourth o' June in comin,
The hour o' Cause, in our Courtha'
At Whiteford's arms, ye answer LAW!

But, as reluctantly we punish,
An' rather, mildly would admonish:
Since Better Punishment prevented,
Tham OBSTINACY sair repented.—
Then, for that *ancient Secret's sake*,
Ye have the honor to partake;
An' for that *noble Badge* you wear,
You, SANDIE DOW, our BROTHER dear,
We give you as a MAN an' MASON,
This private, sober, friendly lesson.—

Your crime, a manly deed we view it.
As *man alone* can only do it;
But, in denial, persevering,
Is to a *Scoundrel's name* adhering.
The best of *men* hae been surpris'd;
The best o' *women* been advis'd:
Nay, *cleverest Lads* hae haen a trick o't,
An' *bonniest Lasses* taen a lick o't.—
Then Brother Dow, if you're asham'd
In such a QUORUM to be nam'd,
Your conduct much is to be blam'd.—
See, ev'n *himsel*—there's godly BRYAN,
The auld *whatreck* he has been tryin;
When such as he put to their han',
What man or character need stan'?
Then Brother dear, lift up your brow,
And, like yoursel, the truth avow;
Erect a dauntless face upon it,
An' say, "I am the man has done it;
"I Sandie Dow gat Meg wi' wean,
"An's fit to do as much again."

Ne'er mind their solemn rev'rend faces,
Had they—in proper times an' places,
But *seen & fun'*—I muckle dread it,
They just would done as you & we did.—
To tell the truth's a manly lesson,
An' doubly proper in a MASON.—
You MONSIEUR BROWN, as it is proven,
Meg Mitchel's wame by you was hoven;
Without you by a quick repentence
Acknowledge Meg's an' your acquaintance,
Depend on't, this shall be your sentence.—
Our Beadles to the Cross shall take you,
And there shall mither naked make you;
Some canie grip near by your middle,
They shall it bind as tight's a fiddle;
The raep they round the pump shall tak
An' tye your hans behint your back;
Wi' just an ell o' string allow'd
To jink an' hide you frae the croud.
There shall ye stan', a legal seizure.
Induring Maggie Mitchel's pleasure;
So be, her pleasure dinna pass
Seven turnings of a half-hour glass:
Nor shall it in her pleasure be
To louse you out in less than three.—
This, our futurum esse DECREET,
We mean it not to keep a secret;
But in OUR SUMMONS here insert it,
And whoso dares, may controvert it.—
This, mark'd before the date and place is;
Subsignum est per B[urns] the Praeses.—

L.S.B.

This summons & the Signet mark
Extractum est per R[ichmon]d, Clerk.—
                                    R . . . . d.
At M[auchli]ne, twenty fifth o' May,
About the twalt hour o' the day,[1]
You two in propria personae
Before design'd Sandie & Johnie,
This SUMMONS legally have got,
As vide witness underwrote;
Within the house of John D[ow], Vintner,
Nunc facio hoc—
                        Gullelmus Hun[te]r.

Have you read these dictionaries in PAPERMAC?

GROSE – **1811 DICTIONARY OF THE VULGAR TONGUE**

Forward by M. Harris £1.95

Did you know that 'pig' was a perjorative word for 'policeman' way back in 1811. A glorious repertoire of cant, underworld idiom and linguisitc surprises.

RADFORD and SMITH **TO COIN A PHRASE**

£2.95

"There I sat, bending the elbow, a bit browned off and out-of-sorts when in walks a toff talking nineteen to the dozen about some junk." A unique analysis of the language we speak.

LE MOT JUSTE

A Dictionary of Foreign and Classical Words and Phrases
£2.95

Do you practise 'Real politik', receive 'billet doux', or play 'jeu de mots'? If you're not sure, then this book will tell you.

KENNETH HUDSON **DICTIONARY OF DISEASED ENGLISH** £2.95

An attack on the monstrous ill-treatment of the English language deformed by "vandals and incompetants".

Available at your local bookseller or send a cheque (with your name and address) payable to **PAPERMAC, Dept JD, 4 Little Essex Street, London WC2.** (Postage and packing free.)

PAPERBACKS FROM MACMILLAN

AUGUST 1914
BARBARA TUCHMAN

Barbara Tuchman's universally acclaimed study of the insane,
uncontrollable plunge into war and the bloody catalogue of the battles of
August 1914 stands as one of the classics of historical writing.   £4.95

*". . . a magnificent achievement, a masterpiece of the
historian's art."* – The Guardian

". . . a brilliant achievement." – Sunday Telegraph

THE PROUD TOWER
A Portrait of the World before the War 1890-1914
BARBARA TUCHMAN

The fateful quarter century leading up to the Great War comes
magnificently to life in these pages. With an artist's eye the author
portrays the splendour and the chaos of the end of an era, the main
figures, movements and moments of time.   £4.95

*"Wonderful, that is the only word for it . . . As a brilliant tour de
force I do not think this can be matched."* – J. H. Plumb

". . . written with remarkable zest . . . infinitely readable . . ."
– A. J. P. Taylor

THE ZIMMERMAN TELEGRAPH
BARBARA TUCHMAN

The interception of a seemingly routine telegram from the German
Foreign Minister to his Ambassador in Mexico in Janaury 1917 changed
the course of the war.   £2.95

"As thrilling as a John Buchan novel." – TLS

Available at your local bookseller or send a cheque, with your name and
address, payable to **PAPERMAC, Dept SR, 4 Little Essex Street,
London WC2** (postage and packing free).

PAPERMAC
PAPERBACKS FROM MACMILLAN

W. B. YEATS
Autobiographies
£3.95

In *Autobiographies* Yeats recalls the people and events that coloured his life; childhood in rural Sligo, literary circles of late-Victorian London, friendship and collaboration with some of the brilliant men of his time – Oscar Wilde, Aubrey Beardsley, J. M. Synge – and the turbulent politics of Ireland under Parnell.

A major literary work in its own right *Autobiographies* is also a vivid portrait of the artistic and political world of late Victorian and Edwardian Britain. Yet, despite its obvious fascination for student and general reader alike, it has never been available in paperback.

W. B. YEATS
A Vision
£3.95

Throughout his life W. B. Yeats was subject to psychic experiences which profoundly affected his thought and inspired much of his most important work. *A Vision* is Yeat's remarkable account of his contact with the supernatural through his wife's 'automatic writing' and 'automatic speech'.

The 'voices' that communicated with her instructed Yeats in a philosophy which seemed to answer his questions about life and art. Over a period of years a complete pattern of metaphors and symbols gradually emerged and it was this which provided Yeats with a framework for much of his greatest and most complex poetry.

Available at your local bookseller or send a cheque, with your name and address, payable to **PAPERMAC, Dept SR, 4 Little Essex Street, London WC2** (postage and packing free).

PAPERBACKS FROM MACMILLAN

THOMAS HARDY
An Illustrated Biography
TIMOTHY O'SULLIVAN

"An excellent guide" – The Sunday Times

A wide range of photographs and some of Hardy's own sketches, illustrate this biography, which captures the spirit of Hardy's beloved Wessex.   **£4.95**

THOMAS HARDY
The Complete Poems

The New Wessex Edition of *The Complete Poems* of Thomas Hardy has been praised by scholars and laymen alike. Now it is available in paperback for the first time, complete with 947 poems, and extensive notes by James Gibson will make a welcome addition to any Hardy lovers library.   **£3.95**

HARDY: *Novelist and Poet*   £3.95
DESMOND HAWKINS

"This is the best single volume treatment of the life, the novels and the poems that one can imagine." – Robert Gittings, Encounter

"Mr Hawkins knows his Wessex almost as well as Hardy himself." – R. C. Churchill, Contemporary Review

Available at your local bookseller or send a cheque (with your name and address) payable to **PAPERMAC, Dept SR, 4 Little Essex Street, London WC2** (postage and packing free).

PAPERBACKS FROM MACMILLAN